W9-CCD-474

Berlitz

Vienna

Cover: Schönbrunn Palace

Right: Johann Strauss the
Younger in the Stadtpark

TOP 10 ATTRACTIONS

Kunsthistorisches Museum
Works by Raphael are among its many masterpieces (page 49)

Schönbrunn Empress Maria Theresa's opulent rococo palace and gardens (page 64)

The Secession Building
Home to Gustav Klimt's 34-m (112-ft) long *Beethoven Frieze* (page 52)

Stephansdom •
The cathedral at the heart of Vienna's Innere Stadt (page 25)

Karlsplatz It has numerous attractions in addition to the Karlskirche (*page 54*)

The Belvedere Among its treasures is Klimt's *The Kiss* (*page 58*)

The Spanish Riding School See the Lipizzaner stallions perform (*page 42*)

The Hofburg Imperial palace of the Habsburgs (*page 40*)

The Prater Vienna's huge expanse of parkland, home to the Riesenrad (*page 68*)

The MuseumsQuartier Where the Museum of Modern Art, Architecture Centre, kids' ZOOM and multimedia exhibitions can all be found (*page 51*)

INTRODUCTION

The elegant Viennese have what is known as *Wiener Lebens-art*, a cultured appreciation of all the pleasures of life. Not only is this reflected in Vienna's glorious art, music and architecture, theatres and coffee houses, and its passion for glittering balls, but where else would you find vineyards within the city's limits? In 2001, the Innere Stadt (Old City) was designated a UNESCO World Heritage Site, a well-deserved honour for an area that embraces baroque palaces, elegant shops, the famous Burgtheater and Staatsoper (Opera House), and a maze of narrow medieval streets winding around the Stephans-

dom (St Stephen's Cathedral). The Innere Stadt isn't the only World Heritage Site in Vienna: Schloss Schönbrunn joined the list in 1996.

Yet Vienna, with a population of 1.5 million, isn't preserved as a museum exhibit. Old places are revamped and given new uses, and various recent constructions, from the whimsy of Hundertwasser's garbage incinerator to the steel Millennium Tower, add a 21st-century dimension. In the historic centre, projects such as the MuseumsQuartier blend old and new to enhance the cityscape.

City districts

Vienna is divided into 23 districts. The 1st District is the historic Innere Stadt (Old City), and districts 2 to 9 fan out around the Ringstrasse.

Left: Schönbrunn Palace facade. Above: Urban transport

A further factor in UNESCO's recognition is that since the 16th century, Vienna has been universally acknowledged as the musical capital of Europe. And the music goes on: you can still hear the waltzes of Johann Strauss – only he could describe the muddy brown Danube as blue. At the Opera House, imagine yourself to be Mozart's Don Giovanni, or one of his beautiful conquests, and then go off to a *Heuriger* wine-garden on the edge of the Vienna Woods for a late-night glass of white wine and a gloriously sentimental song. Or enjoy the beer and something electronic in one of the city's clubs.

Vienna is a town with space to relax, and its rural setting induces a more easygoing attitude to life than that found in other modern cities of comparable size.

Tradition and Modernity

The Viennese are proud of their city's heritage and achieve both continuity and change: they have renovated the grand old hotels and coffee houses, and the clientele – the artists, writers, thinkers and dreamers – have now been joined by TV

The Waltz

Music in Vienna is fuelled not only by its hallowed classical tradition, but also by the joy of its waltzes. The waltz began as a triple-time German traditional dance known as a *Ländler*, which the Viennese transformed into a whirling moment of fairyland. The man who brought the waltz to popular dance halls in 1819 was Joseph Lanner, leader of a small band. He took on a young viola player named Johann Strauss and the waltz took off in a big way. The group grew to become an orchestra and Strauss broke away to form his own – Lanner sadly celebrating the occasion with his *Trennungswalzer (Separation Waltz)*. The two conducted a prolonged 'waltz war' for public favour in the cafés of the Prater. The rivalry ended amicably and Strauss played waltzes – *adagio* – at Lanner's funeral.

The glamorous Opernball, highlight of Vienna's ball season

producers, advertising people and tourists. Viennese fashion designers have taken the time-honoured warm woollen *Loden* fabric and given it a more innovative cut and brighter colours than the traditional olive-green jackets and overcoats. The revered Burgtheater is constantly upsetting its older public with provocative productions by the likes of Thomas Bernhard.

The grandeur of the Habsburg Empire's royal collections includes European masterpieces to enjoy, but Vienna also displays its 20th-century masters – Klimt, Schiele and Kokoschka – who shocked the public of their day.

Vienna offers an astonishing choice of museums, from the sublime to the surprising, from art and high culture to schnapps and reusable coffins (many of these can be visited for free or at reduced rates with the Vienna Card, available from the tourist information office). But some things (thankfully) don't change: *Fiakers* (carriages) still drive tourists around the centre; the pure white Lipizzaner stallions dance

Viennese charm

The Viennese seldom miss an opportunity to make a flattering remark: 'I kiss your hand, Madam' or 'I am honoured'. Even the familiar greeting *Servus* ('hi' or 'bye') is the latin for 'your servant'.

at the Spanish Riding School; the Café Konditorei still presents a delicious array of gateaux, topped by *Sachertorte*, served with coffee; and the ball season remains the focal point of the social calendar. In January and February, the Opernball at the Opera House and the Philharmoniker Ball at the Musikverein vie with one another as the place to see and be seen. Confectioners throw the Zuckerbäckerball and the Kaffeesiederball honours coffee. Doctors, lawyers, even the *Fiaker* cab drivers have their night. Then in May it's the turn of the international celebrities who descend on the city to attend the Life Ball, Europe's largest AIDS charity event.

At the Crossroads

Vienna's historic role as a crossroads of Eastern and Western European civilisation has taken on a new significance since the collapse of the Soviet bloc and Austria's entry into the European Union in 1995. The city's relaxed atmosphere often comes as a surprise to visitors. The Viennese still seem to have time for the courtesies of the old days. Although recent social innovations have been generally popular in Vienna, the people remain profoundly conservative in their values. Politically the Viennese have always been impossible to define. They cheered their Habsburg emperors and then Napoleon. They welcomed the republican experiment after World War I and then hailed Hitler. And then they found democracy rather nice, too. It seemed conducive to their legendary taste for *Gemütlichkeit*. Roughly translated, *gemütlich* means comfy and cosy, the quality that takes the rough edges off life. It is part of the famous Viennese charm, a charm also sharpened by undertones of sometimes malicious irony known as *Wiener Schmäh* (Viennese sarcasm).

As capital of the Habsburg Empire, Vienna was home not only to Slavs and Hungarians, but also to Germans and other Europeans. The Jews, too, such a vital force in pre-1938 Vienna, left their mark on the culture: psychoanalyst Sigmund Freud, composer Gustav Mahler and playwright Arthur Schnitzler among others. Modern Vienna recognises their suffering in the Nazi era. Now, new generations of Poles, Italians, Turks, Croats and other ethnic groups from the former Yugoslavia, as well as from outside Europe, have again swollen the workforce. There is a sizeable group of prosperous, and so more leisurely, Russians. The language is, of course, German, but, like Viennese cuisine, it has that distinctive Viennese way of incorporating elements from the many ethnic groups that make up the city's population.

Vienna, with the Karlskirche

A BRIEF HISTORY

From earliest times, Vienna was a crossroads for people migrating between Eastern and Western Europe. The first identifiable inhabitants of the area were Illyrians who sailed up the Danube from the Balkan peninsula. Celts migrating from Gaul founded the town of Vindobona ('Shining Field') around 500BC.

Romans and Barbarians

The Romans arrived in the 1st century AD. Sent from Britain to defend the empire's eastern European frontier, Rome's soldiers built their garrison in what is today the Inner City's Hoher Markt. They had their work cut out fending off invasions of the Teutons and Slavs. Emperor Marcus Aurelius led the fight against the barbarians, but died in Vindobona of the plague in AD180. A hundred years later, another Roman emperor, Probus, won the gratitude of subsequent generations by developing vineyards on the slopes of the Wienerwald (Vienna Woods). Today, Probusgasse, a street in the heart of the *Heuriger* wine district of Heiligenstadt, honours his initiative.

Christianity arrived in the 4th century, but was powerless against successive waves of barbarian warriors. Attila the Hun advanced on Vienna in 453, but died before completing its conquest. The Huns were followed over the next 600 years by rampaging Goths, Franks, Avars, Slavs and Magyars. Despite these depradations, the first church, Ruprechtskirche, was erected in 740. Two more followed during the reign of Charlemagne: Maria am Gestade and the Peterskirche.

Babenberg Rule

Stability came in 1156 when the Babenbergs, Bavarian lords who had succeeded a century and a half earlier in driving out the Magyars, were granted the hereditary duchy of Austria by the Holy Roman Emperor.

The first duke, Heinrich II Jasomirgott, set up his court around what is today the Platz am Hof, giving Vienna its first golden era. Art, trade and handicrafts thrived, attracting immigrant German merchants and artisans. Vienna became an important stopover for crusaders. Scottish and Irish monks on their way to Jerusalem founded the monastery of Schottenstift. Babenberg rule brought many new churches, notably the first Stephansdom, as well as several monasteries, elegant residences for the nobility along the broad new thoroughfares, and a fortress on the site of the future Hofburg castle. In 1200, financed with English ransom money paid to liberate King Richard the Lion Heart, a ring of fortifications was built around the Innere Stadt, along what is now the Ringstrasse. It was also the great era of the minstrels and the start of Vienna's long musical tradition.

Babenberg family tree at the monastery of Klosterneuburg

The Habsburgs

In 1246, on the death of Friedrich der Streitbare (the Quarrelsome), the male line of the Babenbergs died out and the country fell to Ottokar II of Bohemia. Unlike his predecessor, who had disturbed the city's hard-earned

Obscure origins

For a dynasty that was to supply rulers to Germany, Austria, Hungary, Bohemia, Spain and other states, the Habsburgs had obscure origins. The house took its name from the castle of Habsburg, or Habichtsburg (Hawk's Castle), on the Aar River in present-day Switzerland, built by Werner, Bishop of Strasbourg, and his brother Count Radbot.

peace by picking fights with his barons, seducing the burghers' wives and going off to war at the slightest provocation, Ottokar was popular with the Viennese. He made additions to the Stephansdom and started on the Hofburg. The people did not seem to appreciate that the new German king, Rudolf von Habsburg, had his eye on the city. They supported Ottokar, but in 1278 Rudolf triumphed.

Vienna's history for centuries thereafter was a constant confrontation between the Habsburgs' visions of grandeur and world conquest and the citizens' taste for the quiet life. Whenever the Habsburgs went about their empire-building, under Maximilian I, Karl V and Ferdinand I, Vienna was painfully neglected. The most popular rulers were the ones who chose to stay at home and build things. Rudolf der Stifter (the Founder) created the university in 1365 and turned the Romanesque Stephansdom into the Gothic structure you see today. Friedrich III completed the work and won Rome's approval for Vienna to become a bishopric in 1469. The Viennese showed their appreciation by burying him in the cathedral. As his tomb attests, it was Friedrich who dreamed up the grandiose motto: AEIOU, '*Austriae Est Imperare Orbi Universo*', for which the English translation is 'It falls to Austria to rule the world'.

The 15th century was not all sweetness and light: in 1421, more than 200 Jews were burned alive in their quarter around Judenplatz and the remainder were driven out of the city. The Hungarian king Matthias Corvinus occupied Vienna from 1485 to 1490. He is remembered for his remark: 'Let others wage war while you, happy Austria, arrange marriages. What Mars gives to others, you receive from Venus.' The reference was to the Habsburgs' knack of expanding their empire through judicious mating of their innumerable archdukes and archduchesses, a policy that was used to great advantage by Maximilian I (1493–1519).

Picking up where the Goths and the Magyars left off, the Ottomans under Suleiman the Magnificent staged a crippling 18-day siege of Vienna in 1529. The suburbs were devastated, but the Innere Stadt held fast and the Turks were finally forced to retreat.

In the Reformation of the 16th century and the Thirty Years War that followed, the city emerged as a bulwark of the Catholic Church. Having withstood the Muslim Turks, Vienna banned Protestant worship in 1577, and repelled an attack by the Protestant Swedes of Gustav Adolph in 1645.

Jews were allowed back into town, having been confined during the 1620s to a ghetto on the riverside marshlands of Leopoldstadt. Emperor Leopold I was the one to usher Vienna into its glorious baroque era, a feast of architecture and music that scarcely paused to deal with the vicious plague of

Close-up of the Hofburg Imperial Palace

1679 and another Ottoman siege in 1683. The great soldier and scholar Prince Eugene of Savoy *(see below)* was rewarded for his victory over the Turks with ample funds to build the magnificent and now renowned Belvedere Palace. The Auerspergs, Schwarzenbergs and Liechtensteins followed suit with palaces on a more modest, but equally elegant scale.

Karl VI, pretender to the Spanish throne, returned to Vienna more Spanish than Austrian, bringing with him the strict formality and piety of the Spanish court. His renovation of the 12th-century Abbey Klosterneuburg in baroque style was an attempt to create an Austrian version of El Escorial. Similarly, the huge Karlskirche was originally intended to emulate St Peter's in Rome. Vying with Versailles, the Hofburg Palace underwent a massive expansion which included the building of the Spanish Riding School and the Imperial Library. The transformation of Vienna into a city of the baroque was largely the work of three Austrian architects: Johann Bernhard Fischer von Erlach, his son Josef Emanuel, and Johann Lukas von Hildebrandt.

Prince Eugene of Savoy (1663–1736)

Sceptical by nature, the Viennese have few authentic heroes; ironically, the greatest was a Frenchman who became the supreme Austrian patriot. A unique blend of military courage, culture and human warmth, Prince Eugene of Savoy was born in Paris in 1663. Unsuccessful in establishing a military career in his own country under Louis XIV, the prince spent a period in a monastery and then went to Austria to seek his fortune. He arrived in Vienna in 1683, just in time to help out with the campaigns against the Turks. Over the next 30 years he fought brilliantly for Austria against the Ottomans and the French, rising to the position of commander-in-chief in 1697. Small of stature and always dressed in a rough brown uniform, simple as a monk's, he was known to his soldiers as 'the little Capuchin'.

Maria Theresa and Napoleon

After the feverish construction projects that crowned the empire-building efforts of the male Habsburgs, the Viennese were delighted to be able to relax under the maternal eye of Maria Theresa (1740–80). Pious, warm and sentimental, this mother of 16 children had an unerring feel for the moods of her capital's citizens. She was an enthusiastic patron of the arts, especially music. She loved to

Empress Maria Theresa

have concerts and operas performed at her newly completed Schönbrunn Palace, which she infinitely preferred to the more austere Hofburg. Her orchestra director was Christoph Gluck. Young Joseph Haydn sang in the Vienna Boys' Choir, and six-year-old Wolfgang Amadeus Mozart won Maria Theresa's heart by asking for the hand of one of her daughters. (In the event, the daughter in question, Marie-Antoinette, was destined to lose her head for somebody else.) In the following years, these three composers – Gluck, Haydn and Mozart – launched Vienna's reputation as a city of music.

Maria Theresa lulled the Viennese into a false sense of security. Her son Joseph II (1780–90), very serious-minded and not particularly tactful, shocked them into a reluctant awareness of the revolutionary times that were coming. He rushed through a series of far-reaching reforms, making life easier for peasants, Protestants and Jews. But the conservative Viennese were not ready. They were startled to see him open up the city by tearing down the wall around the Innere

Stadt, and were impressed by the bureaucratic machine he installed to run the empire.

People felt more secure with the cynical and not at all reform-minded Franz II, particularly following the news from France of the execution of Joseph's sister Marie-Antoinette. On seeing the strange tricolour flag hoisted by the new envoy of the French republic, the Viennese promptly tore it to shreds – along with diplomatic relations between Austria and France. They were less bumptious when Napoleon's armies arrived in November 1805 and the French emperor moved into Maria Theresa's beloved Schönbrunn on his way to further glories at Austerlitz.

Once more, the Habsburgs' secret weapon in foreign policy, politically astute marriages, came into play. Now, faced in 1810 with saving what was left of the empire, Emperor Franz did not hesitate to give his daughter Marie-Louise in marriage to his enemy Napoleon. The Viennese did not protest, preferring a quiet life to more war.

The Long 19th Century

The Napoleonic era ended with one of the city's most splendid moments, the Congress of Vienna in 1815, organised by Franz's crafty chancellor, Metternich, for the post-war carving up of Napoleon's Europe. Franz was happy to leave the diplomatic shenanigans to Metternich while he supervised a non-stop spectacle of banquets, balls and concerts. Many considered Franz more successful than Metternich. 'This Congress does not make progress,' said Belgium's Prince de Ligne, 'it dances.'

For the next 30 years or so the city relaxed for a period of gracious living for the middle class and aristocracy, with the Prater park a favourite outing for royalty. And it was time for more music. Beethoven had become the darling of an aristocracy eager to make amends for its shameful neglect of

Mozart. But in general the taste was more for the waltzes of Johann Strauss, both father and son.

In 1848 Vienna became caught up in a wave of revolution that spread across Europe in support of national independence and political reform. Ferdinand, the most sweet-natured but also the most dim-witted of Habsburg emperors, exclaimed when he heard that disgruntled citizens were marching on his Hofburg, 'Are they allowed to do that?' He fled town before getting an answer. The authoritarian Metternich was forced out of power, and the mob hanged the war minister, Theodor Latour, from a lamp-post before imperial troops brutally re-established order.

Ferdinand abdicated and his deadly-earnest nephew, Franz Joseph, took over. Grimly aware of his enormous burden, Franz Joseph concentrated throughout his 68-year reign on defending his family's interests and preserving as much of the

Johann Strauss the Younger commemorated in the Stadtpark

Emperor Franz Joseph

empire as possible. Vienna offered him a paradoxically triumphant arena in which to preside over inevitable imperial decline. Prospering from the Industrial Revolution, the city enthusiastically developed the Ringstrasse, with imposing residences for capitalism's new aristocracy and expanded residential districts for the burgeoning bourgeoisie.

The World Fair in 1873, which nearly bankrupted the city, sang its praises, and people travelled from Europe and America to see the new opera house, concert halls and theatres. The Austrian Empire's cultural achievements were consecrated in monumental form before the empire itself disappeared. Brahms, Bruckner, Mahler, Lehar and Strauss provided the music. At the Secession Gallery, a group of young artists introduced a new style of art, which came to be known as *Jugendstil* (Art Nouveau; *see page 53*). Only a spoilsport like Sigmund Freud over at the university would suggest that the Viennese examine the depths of their unconscious for the seeds of their darker impulses. They, of course, paid no attention. As the intellectuals in the coffee houses clucked disapprovingly, the town waltzed on. A would-be painter named Adolf Hitler left town in disgust at this lack of seriousness, blaming the Jews and Slavs he had encountered in Vienna for the problems of the 'true Germans'.

The End of the Empire

Having lost his son Rudolf through a suicide in Mayerling, and his wife Elisabeth to an assassin's knife in Geneva, Franz Joseph was stricken but fatalistic when he heard that his heir, Archduke Franz Ferdinand, had been shot in Sarajevo. The World War (1914–18) that followed ended the Habsburg Empire and left Vienna in economic ruin. Vienna lost its hinterland of the Czech and Slovak republics, Hungary, parts of Poland, Romania and what was Yugoslavia, all of which had brought it economic prosperity and cultural enrichment.

While the state opera could boast Richard Strauss as its director, and the old creative spirit re-emerged in architecturally progressive public housing, the city suffered from crippling inflation. Politically polarised, street fighting broke out between Communists and Fascist supporters of the government of Engelbert Dollfuss. In 1934 he was assassinated by the outlawed Austrian Nazis in the Chancellery on Ballhausplatz. His successor, Kurt von Schuschnigg, succeeded in crushing the putsch, but was forced four years later to yield to Hitler's *Anschluss* (German annexation) of Austria.

On 13 March 1938, Hitler's triumphant drive along the Mariahilferstrasse was cheered by the Viennese, who saw him as their saviour from the chaos of recent years. He proved the opposite for the city's 180,000 Jews. The brutality of the Austrian Nazis and the spite of many local citizens shocked even those who had witnessed their counterparts at work in Germany. The extermination of the Viennese Jews left a great stain on the city and a gaping hole in its intellectual life and cosmopolitan culture.

No trace

Hitler's residence in the city is not commemorated. It is recorded that he stayed in a hostel at Meldemannstrasse 27 and that he had a flat at Stumpergasse 31. But there isn't anything to see at either site.

In some small measure, the city's spirit survived in World War II. Joseph Bürckel, the Nazi Gauleiter overseeing Vienna, warned Goebbels that it was perhaps better to allow satirical cabaret to continue. However, by the bombardments of 1945 all humour had evaporated. After the war, Vienna, like Berlin, was divided into four sectors, with the Innere Stadt under the joint administration of the Americans, Russians, British and French. The penury was countered by stoic acceptance and a vicious black market.

Austria's post-war neutrality, granted in 1955, made Vienna an appropriate host for the International Atomic Energy Agency, the United Nations Industrial Development Organisation and OPEC. With the status of a world statesman, Chancellor Bruno Kreisky even gave the city a familiar old whiff of international power-broking.

Austria joined the European Union in 1995, once more giving Vienna an active role in Europe. However, with the entry of a far-right party into the governing coalition, the country's reputation for unsavoury political attitudes again came under scrutiny, and the following years saw Austria enact some of the most restrictive immigration laws in the EU. The Viennese still cling firmly to their social-democratic traditions, but Austria is evenly split between left and right and is currently governed by a 'Grosse Koalition'. The far right shows no sign of disappearing, even surviving the death of its populist leader Jörg Haider in a car crash in 2008 by going on to make gains in regional elections in 2009.

Modern Vienna's UNO-City

Historical Landmarks

c. 500BC Celts build town of Vindobona.

1st century AD Romans establish garrison.

4th–9th century Barbarian invasions.

740 Ruprechtskirche is built, the earliest known Christian church.

1156–1246 Babenbergs reign as dukes of Vienna; the first Stephansdom cathedral and precursor of the Hofburg castle is built.

1278 Rudolf von Habsburg launches 640-year dynasty.

1365 University of Vienna founded.

1421 Jewish pogrom; 200 burned to death.

1529 First Turkish siege repelled.

1577 Catholic Church bans Reformation Protestants.

17th century Jews confined to ghetto and then allowed back into town.

1683 Second Turkish siege repelled.

1740–80 Popular Maria Theresa makes her home in Schönbrunn Palace; Haydn and Mozart make Vienna the musical capital.

1780–90 Joseph II's reforms prove unpopular with the Viennese.

1805 Napoleon arrives in Vienna.

1815 The Congress of Vienna carves up Europe while princes dance.

1848 Short-lived revolt drives Metternich from Vienna. Emperor Ferdinand replaced by Franz Joseph (1848–1916).

1873 World Fair celebrates Vienna's grandeur.

1900 Sigmund Freud writes *The Interpretation of Dreams*.

1914–18 Defeat in World War I ends Austrian Empire.

1934 Austrian Nazis assassinate Chancellor Dollfuss.

1938 German annexation *(Anschluss)* of Austria.

1939–45 World War II: Allied bombs devastate city.

1955 Austria granted neutrality.

1995 Austria enters European Union.

1999 Far-right Freedom Party joins a coalition government.

2005 Austria celebrates *Jubiläumsjahr*, the 50th anniversary of the State Treaty and 60th of the Second Republic.

2009 Vienna celebrates the 200th anniversary of Haydn's death.

WHERE TO GO

Nearly all Vienna's major attractions are packed inside the Innere Stadt (Inner City). This means that places such as the Stephansdom (St Stephen's Cathedral), the Hofburg (Imperial Palace), the Burgtheater (National Theatre), Mozart's house, the Staatsoper (State Opera) and the shops on and around Kärntnerstrasse and the Graben are all within walking distance. Even the Kunsthistorisches Museum (Museum of Fine Arts) and Karlskirche are only just outside the Ringstrasse that marks the medieval precincts of the 1st District.

The best way to view the formidable monuments along the Ringstrasse is by **tram** (*Strassenbahn*; tram No. 1 runs around the Ring). Trams also cover some 35 routes to outlying districts and provide a good, cheap way of reaching other parts of the city on your trip, for instance Schönbrunn Palace or a *Heuriger* wine garden. The **U-Bahn** subway system has five lines, numbered U1 to U6 (U5 has not yet been built). U1 and U3 intersect in the city centre at Stephansplatz. The other most conveniently located station is Karlsplatz.

INNERE STADT

Stephansdom

The imposing **Stephansdom** (St Stephen's Cathedral; Mon–Sat 6am–10pm, Sun 7am–10pm; www.stephanskirche.at), located right in the heart of Vienna, is the best place to start a tour. Whichever way you choose to walk through the Innere Stadt you inevitably seem to end up at the cathedral. For more than eight centuries it has watched over Vienna, weathering

Vienna viewed from the steeple of the Stephansdom

Secret code

Painted on the wall just inside the main entrance of the Stephansdom are the characters 05. This is the secret code of an Austrian resistance movement against the Nazis which began in 1944. The 5 stands for the fifth letter of the alphabet, E, and OE (Ö) is the first sound of Österreich (Austria).

city fires, Turkish cannonballs and German and Russian shells. Part of the Stephansdom's charm derives from the asymmetry of its steeple, set to one side. Affectionately known as *Steffl*, it is 137m (449ft) high. Count 343 steps to the **observation platform** at the top, where the view extends northeast to the Czech Republic and southwest to the Semmering Alps.

The main portal takes its name, **Riesentor** (Giant's Gate), from a huge bone found during construction in the 13th century, which was thought to be the shin of a giant drowned in Noah's flood. Scientists subsequently concluded it was the tibia of a mammoth.

With its Romanesque western facade, Gothic tower and baroque altars, the cathedral epitomises Vienna's genius for harmonious compromise, here managing seamlessly to meld the austerity, dignity and exuberance of three architectural styles. The Romanesque origins (1240) are strkingly visible in the breathtaking **Heidentürme** (Heathen Towers) and statuary depicting, among others, a griffin and Samson fighting a lion. Above the entrance are Jesus, the Apostles and a veritable menagerie of dragons, lions, reptiles and birds representing evil spirits to be exorcised by the sanctity of the church.

The mainly Gothic structure we see today was built in the 14th and 15th centuries. To support their petition to have Vienna made a bishopric, the Habsburgs hoped to impress the Pope by adding a second tower. But the city fathers preferred to spend the money on strengthening city fortifications against the Turks and Protestants, so the **North Tower** was never properly completed, just topped off in 1578 with a nicely frivolous Renaissance cupola. From atop the tower (accessible by lift), you have a fine view of the city. In the tower hangs the 20-tonne **Pummerin bell**, a recast version of the one made from the bronze of Turkish cannons captured after the 1683 siege, but destroyed in the wartime fire of 1945. It is rung only on ceremonial occasions such as New Year's Eve.

Inside the church, in the centre aisle, is the charming carved Gothic **pulpit** of Master Anton Pilgram (1455–1515). At the head of the spiral staircase the sculptor has placed the figures of Augustine, Gregory, Jerome and Ambrose, fathers of the Church – and added a sculpture of himself looking through a window under the staircase. No shrinking violet, Pilgram pops up again at the foot of the elaborate stone organ base he built in the north aisle.

Sculptor Master Pilgram at the foot of the organ base

Left of the high altar is the carved wooden **Wiener Neustädter Altar**. To the right is the marble **tomb** of Emperor Friedrich III (died 1493), honoured by the Viennese for having the city made a bishopric and for inventing the *Semmel,* the little bread roll you receive with every meal.

Mass is held at 10.15am on Sunday and holidays (9.30am July and August). There are guided tours and roof walks, as well as tours of the bone-filled catacombs.

Opposite the Stephansdom looms the contrasting **Haas Haus**, a large, curved building whose windows reflect a distorted cathedral. This hinge between Graben and Stephansplatz was erected in 1990 to plans by Hans Hollein. Stephansplatz joins **Stock-im-Eisen-Platz** (literally meaning 'stick set in iron'), a name which refers to a gnarled old tree trunk on the corner of the Graben and Kärntnerstrasse into which journeymen locksmiths arriving in medieval Vienna would drive a nail for good luck. The nails are now protected by a Perspex shield.

Stephansplatz and the Haas Haus

East of Stephansdom

If you're looking for a place to relax after visiting the cathedral, walk east along Rotenturmstrasse to one of the outdoor cafés on **Lugeck**, a pleasant little square where burglars used to be hanged some 300 years ago. Or wander further over to the **Fleischmarkt**, where, at No. 11, you'll find the oldest tavern in Vienna, the **Griechenbeisl** (1490), once frequented by the likes of Mozart, Beethoven, Schubert, Strauss and Mark Twain, as well as by Marx Augustin *(see panel)*.

Du lieber Augustin

This famous Viennese folk song tells the story of a local itinerant bagpiper – Marx Augustin – who, while drunk late at night, fell into a pit filled with the bodies of dead plague victims, and who actually lived to tell the tale.

Around the corner on Grashofgasse, cross the pretty courtyard of the 17th-century **Heiligenkreuzerhof** abbey, one of the Innere Stadt's most attractive corners, to the **Basiliskenhaus** (Schönlaterngasse 7), steeped in medieval superstition. Here a basilisk – half rooster, half lizard – was said to have lived in a well and breathed its poisonous fumes into the drinking water, until one day a baker's apprentice held up a mirror to the monster and scared it to death.

It is a stone's throw over to the **Alte Universität** (Old University, 1365), where young Franz Schubert lived as a member of the Vienna Boys' Choir. The Alte Universität was closed down after student demonstrations in 1848 against the autocratic regime of Metternich, and the hotheads were moved out of the Innere Stadt to academies in the outer districts until a new university was opened in 1884, safely on the outer edge of the Ring.

On Bäckerstrasse, the baroque house of the old Schmauswaberl restaurant (No. 16) served students with leftovers from the Hofburg kitchens. The French lady of letters Madame de Staël lived at the Palais Seilern, and across the street (at No. 7) is a beautiful ivy-covered arcaded Renaissance courtyard.

Cut across the busy Wollzeile to **Domgasse 5**, where, from 1784 to 1787, Wolfgang Amadeus Mozart lived. The house is now a museum, the **Mozarthaus Vienna** (daily 10am–7pm; charge; U-Bahn 1, 3: Stephansplatz; www.mozarthausvienna. at), which was completely revamped and reopened in time for the 250th anniversary celebrations in 2006. Mozart wrote 11 piano concertos here, well as one horn concerto, two quintets, four quartets, three trios, three piano sonatas, two violin sonatas and the opera *The Marriage of Figaro*. Just around the corner, in Rauhensteingasse, the composer struggled to finish the *Requiem* before his early death. His coffin was assigned to an anonymous grave in the St Marxer Friedhof.

Cheer up with a stroll through the **Fähnrichshof** at the corner of Blutgasse and Singerstrasse. This charming complex of artists' studios, galleries, boutiques, apartments and gardens is a triumph of urban renovation from the ruin left by World War II bombs. The nearby **Franziskanerplatz** presents a fine baroque ensemble – an 18th-century fountain with a statue of Moses by Johann Martin Fischer, the elegant **Franziskanerkirche** (Mon–Sat 7.30–11.30am, 2.30–5.30pm) and the Kleines Café, tastefully remodelled by Hermann Czech.

Kärntnerstrasse to Albertinaplatz

Kärntnerstrasse was once the city's main north–south thoroughfare, continuing on through Carinthia (Kärnten) to Trieste on the Adriatic. It has always been the central artery of Viennese social life, perhaps because it joins the sacred and the cultural heart of Vienna – the Stephansdom at one end and the Staatsoper (Opera House) at the other.

The street, which has been transformed into a traffic-free pedestrian zone, is now a bit of a commercial disgrace, disfigured by large signs such as that for Burger King. However, it still contains some of Vienna's historic shops. Most are modern, but the **Lobmeyr** shop (No. 26) dates back to 1823. The Gothic **Malteserkirche** (No. 37) was founded by the crusading Knights Hospitallers.

Just off Kärntnerstrasse, on Neuer Markt, is the **Kapuzinerkirche** (Church of the Capuchin Friars). Beneath it is the 17th-century imperial burial vault, the **Kaisergruft** (daily 10am–6pm; charge; www.kaisergruft.at), also known as the Kapuzinergruft. Among the tombs and sarcophagi of some 140 Habsburgs, note the double casket of Maria Theresa and her husband, François de Lorraine. The most recent burial was in 1989, of Zita, wife of the last emperor, Karl I (who abdicated in 1918 and is buried in Madeira). Franz Joseph and Empress Elisabeth (Sissi) are apparently still

Lobmeyr on Kärntnerstrasse

much loved, their coffins festooned with flowers.

On Philharmonikerstrasse is the **Hotel Sacher**, which opened in 1882. Anna Sacher, who presided over its early days, was a renowned hostess, anticipating her guests' every need. She attracted courtiers, aristocrats, diplomats and the rich, even embroidering their signatures on a tablecloth. The famous chocolate cake, the *Sachertorte*, is actually 50 years older than the hotel; it was created by Franz Sacher in 1832 for Prince Metternich when he wanted something new and impressive for an important occasion.

At the intersection of Kärntnerstrasse and the Ringstrasse stands the **Staatsoper** (Opera House; guided tours at 1, 2 and 3pm; charge). The original Opera House, inaugurated in 1869, was greeted with such criticism that one of the architects, Edward van der Null, was driven to suicide. It was almost completely destroyed in the 1945 bombardments, but reconstructed to the original design.

The Staatsoper has its own small **museum** (Goethegasse 1; Tue–Sun 10am–6pm) close by – a map is posted on the side of the Opera House – that has displays on past productions. But more can be found out about its orchestra, from which the Wiener Philharmoniker is derived, at the nearby **Haus der Musik** (Seilerstätter 30; daily 10am–10pm; charge; U-Bahn 1, 3: Oper; tram 1, 2, D: Schwarzenberg Platz; www.hdm.at). It is pread over three floors, of which the first has a display on the history of the Wiener Philharmoniker, with a 'compose your own waltz' game. Upstairs is the **Klangmuseum**, an exploration of sound with fun interactive exhibits. The third floor has displays on some of the most famous composers to work in Austria.

Just beside the Staatsoper is **Albertinaplatz**. On the far side of the square is the Lobkowitz Palace, now home to the **Österreichisches Theatermuseum** (partly closed for renovation; Tue–Sun 10am–6pm; charge; U-Bahn 1, 2, 4: Karlsplatz; U-Bahn 1, 3: Oper; tram 1, 2, J, 62, 65: Oper; www.khm.at). Inside are models of theatres, costumes and set designs, as well as the beautifully decorated Eroica Saal where Beethoven's Third Symphony was first performed.

Also on Albertinaplatz is the bleak **Monument against War and Fascism** (1991) by Alfred Hrdlicka. Facing the stone gate symbolising totalitarian force is the controversial bronze sculpture of a kneeling figure, recalling the humiliation of Jews forced by the Nazi regime to scrub pavements with a toothbrush.

Opposite the monument is the **Albertina**, the Habsburg palace that contains the **Graphische Sammlung Albertina** (Albertinaplatz 1; daily 10am–6pm, Wed 9pm; charge;

www.albertina.at). Named after Maria Theresa's son-in-law, Duke Albert of Saxony-Teschen, and founded in 1781, this palace holds one of the world's finest collections of graphic art, with more than 60,000 original drawings and over a million wood and copper-plate prints. The collection represents major artists from the 15th century to the present, including priceless works by Dürer, da Vinci, Michelangelo, Raphael, Titian, Rembrandt, Rubens, Van Gogh, Toulouse-Lautrec, Beardsley and Grosz.

The state rooms have been restored and a new exhibition space created together with storage and retrieval facilities. Any of the drawings can be viewed by written request.

Just below the Albertina, with its entrance on Albertinaplatz, is the newly renovated **Filmmuseum** (www. filmmuseum.at).This puts on a full schedule of art-house and historical films, many taken from its huge archive.

Monument against War and Fascism on Albertinaplatz

The Graben and the Jewish Quarter

Running northwest from Stephansplatz *(see page 25)*, the Graben, together with the adjacent Kohlmarkt and Dorotheergasse, is the centre of Vienna's most fashionable shops and coffee houses. Until the end of the Habsburgs, it was equally infamous for its Graben nymphs, as the local ladies of the night were known. The Graben and its extension, Naglergasse, mark the southern boundary of the original Roman settlement of Vindobona; the approximate square shape is completed by Rotenturmstrasse to the east, Salzgries to the north and Tiefer Graben to the west.

The Graben is now a pedestrian zone, dominated by the startling, bulbous-shaped monument to the town's deliverance from the plague in 1679. The **Pestsäule** (Plague Column) combines humility before God and gruesome fascination with the disease itself. A more joyous celebration of faith, just off the Graben, is the **Peterskirche** (St Peter's Church; Mon–Fri 7am–7pm, Sat–Sun 9am–7pm), designed in 1702 by Gabriele Montani and completed by Johann Lukas von Hildebrandt. The exterior embraces the graceful oval of its nave, its rows of pews curving outwards, each decorated with three carved angels' heads. It displays the genius of Viennese baroque for marrying the sumptuous with the intimate.

Ornate corner near the Graben

South of Stephansplatz, at Dorotheergasse 11, is the **Jüdisches Museum** (Jewish Museum; Sun–Fri 10am–6pm; charge; U-Bahn 1, 3: Stephansplatz; www.jmw.at). This comparatively recent (1993) addition to the Vienna museum scene is housed

The oval nave of the 18th-century Peterskirche

in the 18th-century Palais Eskeles, formerly the property of a prominent Jewish financier. It traces the history of the city's Jewish community from the Middle Ages, through the years of its illustrious contributions to Viennese culture, to its extermination by German and Austrian Nazis in World War II. Temporary exhibitions are also staged here, usually devoted to prominent artists, writers and other historical figures of Viennese life. Despite the community's tragic end, the museum's atmosphere is positive, reinforced by a cheerful café and bookshop on the ground floor.

The old **Jewish Quarter**, still in large part a garment district, lies north of Stephansplatz and the Graben. Its medieval centre was **Judenplatz** (Jews' Square) until the program of 1421 *(see page 14)*, when the synagogue was dismantled and its stones carted off to build an extension to the Alte Universität. The remains of the synagogue have been excavated and now form part of the elaborate **Museum Judenplatz Wien**

(Sun–Thur 10am–6pm, Fri 10am–2pm; charge), which was unveiled in 2000 and functions as an annexe to the Jüdisches Museum on Dorotheergasse *(see page 34)*. On the square is Rachel Whiteread's **Memorial to the Victims of the Holocaust**, which commemorates more than 65,000 Austrian Jews who were killed by the Nazis and is designed to resemble a library turned inside out, so shelves of closed books face inwards.

The one **synagogue** out of the city's 24 that survived the Nazis' 1938 *Kristallnacht* pogrom is at Seitenstettengasse 4, next to a kosher restaurant (guided tours Mon–Thur 11am and 3pm; a combined ticket for the museums allows you to view the synagogue free). With its Jewish community centre, it stands behind an apartment block beside the unusual **Kornhäuselturm** (1827), studio and home of architect Josef Kornhäusel. Inside is a drawbridge he pulled up whenever he wanted to shut himself off from his quarrelsome wife.

Memorial to the Victims of the Holocaust

Around the corner is the city's oldest church, the ivy-covered Romanesque **Ruprechtskirche** (Mon–Thur 10am–noon, Fri 10am–noon, 3–5pm), which is dedicated to Rupert, patron saint of salt – a valuable commodity in earlier times. From here, cut back through Judengasse to the **Hoher Markt**. This was once the forum of Roman Vindobona, and a small museum at No. 2 (Tue–Sun 9am–6pm; charge; www.wienmuseum.at) shows remains of two Roman houses laid bare by a 1945 bombardment. At the east end of the square is a gem of high Viennese kitsch, the **Ankeruhr**, an animated clock built in 1911 by an insurance company. Charlemagne, Prince Eugene, Maria Theresa, Joseph Haydn and others perform their act at midday.

At the western end of Hoher Markt, turn right into Marc Aurel-Strasse, named after the Roman emperor who died in AD180. On the left, Salvatorgasse leads behind the **Altes Rathaus** (Old Town Hall), which now contains the **Archive of the Austrian Resistence** (Mon–Thur 9am–5pm; www.doew.at), and past the superb porch of the **Salvatorkapelle**, a happy marriage of Italian Renaissance and Austrian late Gothic sculpture. Beyond it is the slender 14th-century Gothic church of **Maria am Gestade** (Mary on the Banks), originally overlooking the Danube. Notice its delicate tower, the canopied porch, and remains of Gothic stained glass in the choir.

Platz am Hof

Walk back across the Judenplatz to the spacious **Platz am Hof**, the largest square in the old part of the city. The Babenberg dukes, predecessors of the Habsburgs, built their fortress here in about 1150. It was both a military stronghold and a palace for festivities such as the grand state reception in 1165 for German emperor Friedrich Barbarossa. The **Mariensäule** (Virgin's Column) was erected in 1667 to celebrate victory over Sweden's armies in the Thirty Years War. It was on a lamppost in the middle of this square that the revolutionaries of 1848 hanged war minister Theodor Latour. It was at the baroque **Am Hof** church that the end of the Holy Roman Empire, said by some to be neither holy nor Roman nor an empire, was proclaimed with fanfare in 1806.

Along the narrow street to the left of the church is the **Uhrenmuseum** (Clock Museum; Tue–Sun 10am–6pm; charge; www.wienmuseum.at). Set in one of the oldest buildings in Vienna, with a lovely spiral staircase, it has some interesting exhibits, including the huge workings of the original clock for Stephansdom (1699) and the 18th-century astronomical clock made by the German watchmaker David Cajetano.

Around Herrengasse

In Bognergasse, notice the pretty *Jugendstil* facade of the **Engel-Apotheke** (1907) before returning to medieval Vienna through narrow, cobbled Naglergasse. This leads to the **Freyung** triangle, flanked by the Palais Harrach dating from 1690 (where Joseph Haydn's mother was once the family cook; now a venue for temporary exhibitions mounted by the Kunsthistorisches Museum) and the **Schottenkirche** (Church of the Scots), founded by Scottish and Irish Benedictine monks in the 12th century, whose monastery has an excellent **picture gallery** (Thur–Sat 11am–5pm; charge; www.schottenstift.at).

To the north of the Freyung, just before the Ringstrasse, Schottengasse leads to the Mölker Bastei and the **Pasqualatihaus** (Tue–Sun 10am–1pm, 2–6pm; charge; U-Bahn 2, 4,

Art forum

At Freyung 8, the **Kunstforum der Bank Austria** (Sat–Thur 10am–7pm, Fri 10am–9pm; charge; www.bankaustria-kunstforum.at) mounts first-class exhibitions of contemporary art and sculpture, and paintings from the 19th and 20th centuries.

tram 1, 2: Schottentor; www.wienmuseum.at). Beethoven lived in this house on several occasions between 1803 and 1815 at the invitation of his friend and patron, Baron Johann Baptist of Pasqualati. Here he composed parts of *Fidelio* and his Fourth to Seventh symphonies, as well as his Piano Concerto in G-major (Opus 58). Today it is one of three Beethoven residences in Vienna open to the public as museums *(see also pages 71 and 73).*

Relaxing in Café Central

South of the Freyung is Herrengasse, the Innere Stadt's main eastbound traffic artery, lined with imposing baroque and neo-baroque palaces, now government offices or embassies. Here, too, is the 18th-century **Palais Ferstel**, incorporating an elegant shopping arcade, Freyung Passage, and the restored **Café Central**, Vienna's leading coffee house before World War I *(see page 95).* Upstairs, a restaurant occupies the gilded premises of the old stock exchange.

Herrengasse leads to Michaelerplatz and the Hofburg *(see page 40).* Once the imperial parish church, **Michaelerkirche** (daily 7am–10pm) is a hybrid mixture of Romanesque, Gothic and baroque. At No. 5 is the architecturally revolutionary **Looshaus**, now a bank. Built by Adolf Loos, its starkly functional use of fine materials shocked many in 1910. Emperor Franz Joseph so hated its 'outrageously naked' facade that he stopped using the Hofburg's Michaelertor exit.

Sissi with stars in her hair, by Franz Xaver Winterhalter

THE HOFBURG

Defeat in war took away the Habsburgs, but not the palaces. The most imposing is the **Hofburg** (Michaelerplatz 1; U-Bahn 2: Babenbergerstrasse or Herrengasse; tram 1, 2, D, J: Burgring), home of Austria's rulers since the 13th century.

Covering the southwest corner of the Innere Stadt, the vast palace went through five major stages of construction over six centuries, and at the end there was still a large unfinished section. Today, the palace's museums exhibit most of the vast personal fortune of the Habsburgs.

Imperial Apartments

To sense the human scale of the gigantic enterprise, start by taking the 45-minute guided tour of the **Kaiserappartements** (Imperial Apartments; daily Sept–June 9am–5.30pm, July–Aug 9am–6pm; charge; www.hofburg-wien.at). Coming from the Michaelerplatz, the entrance is to the left of the Hofburg rotunda. You will see splendid Gobelins tapestries; a smoking room for the emperor's fellow officers; enormous rococo stoves needed to heat the place; a crystal chandelier weighing half a tonne; Franz Joseph's austere bedroom with iron military camp-bed; and rooms used by his wife, Elisabeth (Sissi), including her newly restored drawing room and bedroom, and the gymnasium she used for daily exercise, complete with wall bars and climbing ropes.

The first six rooms, the so-called Stephansappartement, are devoted to the **Sissi Museum**. This examines the life of the empress from her carefree childhood in Bavaria to her murder at the hands of an anarchist in Geneva. Particular emphasis is placed on the private life of Elisabeth, including her obsessive exercise regimes and fixation with beauty.

Silver Collection

To the right of the Hofburg rotunda coming from the Michael-erplatz is the **Hofsilber und Tafelkammer** (Imperial Silver and Tableware Collection; same times as the Imperial Appartments). On display are the priceless Chinese, Japanese, French Sèvres and German Meissen services amassed by the Habsburgs over six centuries of weddings and birthdays. Highlights include a

The Life and Death of an Empress

Elisabeth, affectionately known as Sissi, was a Bavarian princess and a legend both in her own lifetime and more than a century after her death. She married Emperor Franz Joseph 1 in 1854 when she was just 16. She was never at home with the oppressive formality of court life, but her presence still made the court the most glittering in Europe. She was noted for her stringent exercise and beauty regime. Hair care took hours, and Elisabeth's hairdresser was a confidante who sometimes took her mistress's place during boring functions where the empress would not be closely scrutinised.

As she grew older, Sissi was able to lead her own life, travelling extensively. She loved the imperial train. In 1898, at the age of 60, she was fatally stabbed by an Italian anarchist in Geneva. In Austria and Hungary she is still a figure of enchantment. A Winterhalter portrait of Sissi with stars in her hair, old romantic films and, most recently, a musical about her life have, perhaps, kept memories green.

140-piece service in vermeil and a neo-Renaissance centrepiece given to Emperor Franz Joseph by Queen Victoria in 1851.

The Stallburg

In 1533, four years after the Turks were repulsed, Ferdinand I felt safe enough to settle in the Hofburg, bringing his barons and bureaucrats to make their homes in nearby Herrengasse and Wallnerstrasse. He built the **Stallburg** in 1565 (outside the main Hofburg complex on

A Lipizzaner performing at the Spanish Riding School

Reitschulgasse) as a home for his son Archduke Maximilian, subsequently turned into stables for the Spanish Riding School. With its fine three-storey arcaded courtyard, the Stallburg is the most important Renaissance building in Vienna. After an outbreak of infection some years ago the stables are no longer open to the public, but visitors can see into six of the 68 stalls from behind a glass screen in the **Lipizzaner Museum** next door (daily 9am–6pm; charge).

Spanish Riding School

Part of the massive expansion of the Hofburg that took place in the 17th and 18th centuries is the magnificent parade hall of the **Winterreitschule**, home of the **Spanische Reitschule** (Spanish Riding School), right opposite the Stallburg. It is worth visiting on architectural grounds alone: constructed between 1729 and 1735, it is the work of Josef Emanuel Fischer von Erlach and is considered a masterpiece of the baroque.

The Lipizzaner horses perform in its elegant arena throughout the year, except in July and August. Tickets must be booked well in advance (Tue–Sat 9am–5pm, Sun 9am–1.30pm; charge; www.srs.at; performances can be booked in advance online, and the daily schedule is posted on leaflets outside the entrance under the Michaelertor). A cheaper option is to watch the horses train. Morning exercises are held between 10am and noon Tuesday to Saturday except in July and August (tickets available on the day from 9am).

The Lipizzaners, originally a Spanish breed, were raised at Lipica in Slovenia, not far from Trieste; since 1920 the tradition has been carried on in the Styrian town of Piber. Using methods unchanged since the 17th century, the horses are trained to perform complex steps and dances.

The Great Hall of the National Library

National Library

Beside the Spanish Riding School complex is **Josefsplatz**, a marvellously harmonious baroque square, in the middle of which stands Franz Anton Zauner's equestrian statue (1795–1807) of Emperor Joseph II.

Behind is the main building of the **Österreichische Nationalbibliothek** (Austrian National Library), which contains more than 2 million manuscripts and printed books, as well as

The Vienna Boys' Choir sings in the Schweizerhof

maps, portraits, musical scores, papyrus documents and a globe museum. The building – the former Imperial Library – is one of the most important works of the court architect Johann Bernhard Fischer von Erlach; it was constructed between 1723 and 1735 under the supervision of his son, Josef Emanuel. The highlight is the **Prunksaal** (Great Hall; Tue–Wed, Fri–Sun 10am–6pm, Thur 10am–9pm; charge; www.onb.ac.at), one of the world's greatest secular baroque interiors. The ceiling frescoes (1730) by Daniel Gran depict the apotheosis of the library's founder, Emperor Charles VI.

The baroque **Augustinerkirche** was the Habsburgs' wedding church. It was here that Maria Theresa married François of Lorraine in 1736, Marie-Louise married Napoleon *(in absentia)* in 1810, and Franz Joseph married Elisabeth in 1854. Although the Habsburgs' burial church is the Kapuzinerkirche over on Neuer Markt *(see page 31)*, the heart of the deceased was buried deep in the Augustiner crypt.

Schweizerhof

The **Schweizerhof** (Swiss Court), the oldest part of the Hofburg, is named after the Swiss Guard once housed there. Here King Ottokar of Bohemia built a fortress in 1275 to resist Rudolf von Habsburg. Victorious Rudolf moved in and strengthened the fortifications to keep out the unruly Viennese. By the archway are the pulleys for the chains of the drawbridge. But Rudolf's son, Albrecht I, preferred the safety of Leopoldsberg in the Vienna Woods. For 250 years, the fortress was used only for ceremonial occasions. The **Burgkapelle** (Castle Chapel; Sept–June Mon–Thur 11am–3pm, Fri 11am–1pm; charge) was built in 1449. Originally Gothic, it was redone in baroque style and then partially restored to its original form in 1802.

In the Schweizerhof, the **Schatzkammer** (Treasury; Wed–Mon 10am–6pm; charge; www.khm.at) contains a dazzling display of the insignia of the old Holy Roman Empire. Highlights are the imperial crown of pure unalloyed gold set with pearls and unpolished emeralds, sapphires and rubies. First used in AD962 for the coronation of Otto the Great in Rome, it moved on to Aachen and Frankfurt for crowning successors. Also on display are the sword of Charlemagne and the Holy Lance, which is said to have pierced the body of

Vienna Boys' Choir

The Wiener Sängerknaben (Vienna Boys' Choir) was founded in 1498 as part of the Imperial Chapel choir with 16 to 20 choirboys. It increased steadily in size over the years, and in the 18th and 19th centuries included Josef Haydn and Franz Schubert among its members. Re-established in 1924, it today consists of four individual choirs, each having 24 members. The choir sings Mass on Sunday and Church festivals in the Burgkapelle (book in advance; fax: 01-533 5067; www.wsk.at).

Christ on the Cross and which has been claimed by some, including Hitler, to have mystical powers. Other intriguing artefacts include a unicorn's horn and an agate bowl, reputed to be the Holy Grail used by Christ at the Last Supper.

The imperial crown

In der Burg

The Schweizertor (Swiss Gate) leads into the busy square known as **In der Burg**, which is surrounded by buildings from various eras. Leopold I launched the city's baroque era with his **Leopoldinischer Trakt** (Leopoldine Wing) – a residence in keeping with the Habsburgs' role as a world power. Constructed in 1660–66 by Domenico and Martin Carlone, to a design by Philiberto Luchesi, it serves today as the official residence of the president of Austria.

The **Amalienburg**, which was started under Emperor Maximilian II in the early baroque style, was finished in 1611 during the reign of Emperor Rudolf II by Pietro Ferrabosco and Antonio de Moys. It was named after Amalia of Brunswick, the consort of Emperor Joseph I.

The **Reichskanzleitrakt** housed the imperial administration until 1806. It was designed by Johann Lukas von Hildebrandt and Josef Emanuel Fischer von Erlach between 1723 and 1730; the four sculptures *(The Labours of Hercules)* are the work of Lorenzo Mattielli, who was active at the same time.

Neue Burg

A passage leads from In der Burg to spacious **Heldenplatz** (Heroes' Square). At the end of the 19th century, Franz

Joseph embarked on building a gigantic Kaiser Forum. This was to have embraced the vast Heldenplatz with two crescent-shaped arms, the whole extending through triumphal arches to the Naturhistorisches and Kunsthistorisches museums. Only the first of the two crescents, the **Neue Burg**, was built before the empire collapsed. Today, it houses a congress centre, several museums, and reading rooms for the National Library.

It contains perhaps the most Viennese of all collections in the Hofburg, the exquisite **Sammlung alter Musikinstrumente** (Musical Instruments Collection; Wed–Mon 10am–6pm; charge), comprising some 360 pieces, including Renaissance instruments representing practically everything played up to the 17th century. Also on display are Haydn's harpsichord, Beethoven's piano of 1803 and an 1839 piano used by Schumann and Brahms.

Statue of Eugene of Savoy on Heldenplatz

The other museums in the Neue Berg are the **Hofjagd-und Rüstkammer** (Collection of Arms and Armour; Wed–Mon 10am–6pm; www.khm.at) and the **Ephesos-Museum** (same times), with exhibits from excavations at the site in Turkey. The star attraction when it fully reopens after a lengthy renovation will be the **Museum für Völkerkunde** (same

Statue of Mozart in the Burggarten

times for temporary exhibitions), the ethnographic collections of the Habsburgs.

The Burggarten

The **Burggarten**, the Hofburg's park, was laid out for the imperial family in the early 19th century. It has monuments to Franz Joseph I (1908, by Klimbusch) and Mozart (1896, by Viktor Tilgner), the latter moved here from Albertinaplatz in 1953. There is also the early 20th-century *Jugendstil* Palmenhaus (Glass House) by Friedrich Ohmann. This contains a lovely café, and the Schmetterlinghaus, a butterfly garden (Apr–Oct Mon–Fri 10am–4.45pm, Sat–Sun 10am– 6.15pm, Nov–Mar daily 10am–3.45pm; www. schmetterling haus.at).

RINGSTRASSE AND ITS MUSEUMS

After the Hofburg, take a walk (or tram ride) around the Ringstrasse, the single urban achievement of Franz Joseph I. This boulevard, encircling the Innere Stadt, was created in the 1860s along the route of the old city walls.

Start west of the Schottenring, at the **Votivkirche** (Tue–Sat 9am–1pm, 4–6.30pm, Sun 9am–1.30pm), a neo-Gothic church built after Franz Joseph survived an assassination attempt in 1853. Next to it are the university and **Rathaus** (Town Hall). Proceed along Dr-Karl-Lueger-Ring, and on the Innere Stadt side is the imposing **Burgtheater** *(see page*

85), a high temple of German theatre. Beyond is the lovely **Volksgarten**, with its small buildings and scaled-down copy of the Athenian Temple of Theseus. Its cafés and concerts carry on a tradition that began with the café music of the Strauss family.

Opposite is the temple-like **Parlament**, built by Theophil Hansen after a long stay in Athens. The ring bends to become the Burg Ring, flanked on the Innere Stadt side by the Hofburg and on the other side by **Maria-Theresien-Platz**, which lies between the Kunsthistorisches Museum and Naturhistorisches Museum.

Kunsthistorisches Museum

If the **Kunsthistorisches Museum** (Museum of Fine Arts; Tue–Wed, Fri–Sun 10am–6pm, Thur 10am–9pm; charge; U-Bahn 2: Babenbergerstrasse; tram 1, 2, D, J: Burgring;

Maria-Theresien-Platz and the Kunsthistorisches Museum

Madonna of the Meadows,
by Raphael

wheelchair access Burgring 5; www.khm.at) is less well known than the Louvre or the Prado, it may just be that the name is something of a mouthful. The collection is, quite simply, magnificent. Benefiting from the cultural diversity of the Habsburg Empire, it in fact encompasses a much broader spectrum of Western European art than many of its better-known counterparts. The **Gemäldegalerie** (Gallery of Paintings) on the first floor displays a dazzling array of European art from the 16th to 18th centuries. Dutch, Flemish, German and English works are in the east wing, left of the main entrance, and Italian, Spanish and French works in the west wing, to the right. Whatever your taste, you can't fail to be awestruck: there are masterpieces by Caravaggio, Dürer, Raphael, Rembrandt, Rubens, Titian, Velázquez, Vermeer, and an entire room devoted to Pieter Brueghel.

The lower floor contains an impressive, and beautifully displayed, collection of ancient Egyptian, Greek and Roman art, as well as the **Sculpture and Applied Arts Collection** (currently closed for renovation), whose prized possession is Benvenuto Cellini's famous gold-enamelled **salt cellar** made for King François I of France. A highlight of the **Classical Antiquities Collection** is the exquisite **Gemma Augustea**, a 1st-century AD onyx cameo. The **Egyptian/Oriental Collection** contains, among other treasures, the burial chamber of Prince Kaninisut.

Naturhistorisches Museum

The architectural twin of the Kunsthistorisches Museum stands opposite: the **Naturhistorisches Museum** (Natural History Museum; Thur–Mon 9am–6.30pm, Wed 9am–9pm; charge; U-Bahn 2, 3: Volkstheater; tram 1, 2, D, J: Dr Karl-Renner-Ring; www. nhm-wien.ac.at). The museum contains exhibits ranging from insects to dinosaurs, and an impressive collection of meteorites. The vast reserves derive in part from the private collections of François of Lorraine (1708–65), husband of Maria Theresa. Highlights include the 25,000-year-old figurine *The Venus of Willendorf*, a 117kg (260lb) giant topaz, and Maria Theresa's exquisite jewel bouquet made of precious stones.

The Leopold Museum in the MuseumsQuartier

MuseumsQuartier

At the other side of Museumstrasse is the modern museum complex, the **Museums Quartier** (Visitor and Ticket Centre, Museumsplatz, daily 10am–7pm; U-Bahn 2, 3: Volkstheater; www.mqw.at). Comprising Fischer von Erlach's 18th-century former Hofstallungen (Imperial Stables) alongside stunning new buildings, it is home to **MUMOK** (Museum of Modern Art, Tue–Wed, Fri–Sun 10am–6pm, Thur 10am–9pm; charge; www.mumok. at), with its fine collection of

20th-century work by artists such as Kandinsky, Magritte and Warhol; the superb **Leopold Museum** (Fri–Wed 10am–6pm, Thur 10am–9pm; charge; www.leopoldmuseum. org), featuring an array of Austrian art from the 19th and 20th centuries, including works by Klimt, Schiele and Max Oppenheimer; and the **Architekturzentrum Wien** (Vienna Architecture Centre; daily 10am–7pm; www.azw.at), which, aside from a nice café, holds temporary exhibitions. Contemporary art exhibitions are on show in the **Kunsthalle Wien** (Fri–Wed 10am–7pm, Thur 10am–10pm; charge; www.kunsthallewien.at). The **ZOOM Kindermuseum** is devoted to interactive education (book at least 24 hours in advance; tel: 01-524 7908; Mon–Fri 8am–4pm, Sat–Sun 9.30am–3.30pm; charge; www.kindermuseum.at).

Fine Arts Academy

The Ringstrasse bends round to become the Opern Ring. On the right is Schillerplatz, home to the **Akademie der Bildenden Künste** (Academy of Fine Arts; Tue–Sun 10am–6pm; charge; U-Bahn 1, 2, 4: Karlsplatz/Oper; tram 1, 2, D, J: Burgring; www.akademiegalerie.at). Few art academies can rival its outstanding collection of European paintings – particularly Dutch and Flemish masters – from the 14th century to the present day. Highlights include *The Last Judgement* by Hieronymus Bosch and works by Rubens, Rembrandt, Van Dyck, Pieter de Hooch and Tiepolo. The building itself was constructed in the 1870s to an Italian Renaissance design by Theophil Hansen.

Secessionsgebäude

Standing defiantly opposite, on the corner of Friedrichstrasse, is the distinctive **Secessionsgebäude** (Secession Building; Tue–Wed, Fri–Sun 10am–6pm, Thur 10am–8pm; charge; U-Bahn 1, 2, 4: Karlsplatz; tram 1, 2, D, J: Burgring; www.

secession.at). This is the gallery of the Secession Movement, which was formed when 19 artists (the most celebrated being Gustav Klimt) broke from what they saw as the reactionary Viennese art establishment in 1897. It was built by Josef Maria Olbrich, a student of Otto Wagner. An inscription above the door proclaims: *'Der Zeit ihre Kunst, der Kunst ihre Freiheit'* ('To the Age, its own Art; to Art, its

The Secession Building

Jugendstil

In Austria, *Jugendstil* (art nouveau) caught the imagination of the art world, and the result was the foundation of the Secession Movement by a group of renegade artists from the Academy in 1897. The central figure of the Secession was Gustav Klimt (1862–1918), whose erotic, fairytale-like painting and themes came to embody *Jugendstil*. One of the key tenets for artists such as Klimt and Koloman Moser, and the leading *Jugendstil* architects Otto Wagner and Josef Hoffmann, was the linking of function and aesthetic.

Klimt's decorative elegance was a particular source of inspiration for Egon Schiele (1890–1918), whose linearity and subtlety reveals the strong influence of the *Jugendstil*. Schiele, however, emphasised expression over decoration, concentrating on the human figure with an acute eroticism that was less decorative than Klimt's. Evocation of intense feeling through colours and lines was of equal importance to Oskar Kokoschka (1886–1980), a leading exponent of Expressionism.

Stadtbahn Pavilion by Secession architect Otto Wagner

own Freedom'). The building is topped with a golden dome of laurel leaves, known locally as the 'golden cabbage', and said to symbolise the interdependence of art and nature. Contemporary work is also on show. In the basement is Klimt's large *Beethoven Frieze*, created for a Secession exhibition in 1902.

Karlsplatz

There are a number of attractions on and around nearby **Karlsplatz**. The elegant glass cube on Treitlstrasse is the **Kunsthalle Project Space** (Sun–Mon 1–7pm, Tue–Sat 4pm–midnight; charge; U-Bahn 1, 2, 4: Karlsplatz; www.kunsthallewien. at), a branch of the Kunsthalle Wien (in the MuseumsQuartier), which stages exhibitions featuring topical themes and current trends in contemporary art. The café, with its giant terrace, is a great meeting place.

The square is dominated by the huge **Karlskirche** (Mon–Sat 9am–6pm, Sun midday–5.45pm; charge; www.karls kirche.at), the most important of the city's baroque churches. It was built by Fischer von Erlach for Karl VI, fulfilling an oath made by the emperor during the plague of 1713. Sunset offers a spectacular view of the big dome across Karlsplatz. The cool, sober interior has a subdued marble decor and spacious oval ground plan similar to that of the Peterskirche *(see page 34)*. The oval dome's ceiling **frescoes** are by Johann Michael Rottmayr, the *trompe-l'oeil* by Gaetano Fanti. Notice, too, Daniel Gran's lovely painting of **St Elisabeth** in the main chapel on the right. In front of the church, Henry Moore's sculpture *Hill Arches* provides a striking contrast.

At the eastern end of Karlsplatz is **Wien Museum Karlsplatz** (Tue–Sun 9am–6pm; charge; U-Bahn 1, 2, 4: Karlsplatz; www.wienmuseum.at). Displays cover the major historical events in the city, from the siege of 1529 to *fin de siècle* artistic movements, including a re-creation of the living room of architect Adolf Loos. There are fascinating models of the city before and after the development of the Ringstrasse.

Opposite is the magnificent neoclassical building of the **Musikverein** (Society of the Friends of Music, *see page 83*; check website for guided tour dates and times; www.musikverein.at). Constructed in 1867 to a design by Theophil Hansen, it is home to the world-famous Vienna Philharmonic Orchestra. The ceiling paintings, *Apollo and the Nine Muses* (1911), are by August Eisenmenger.

The Musikverein

Beside the Musikverein lies the **Künstlerhaus** (1868), which houses art exhibitions (Fri–Wed 10am–6pm, Thur 10am–9pm; www.k-haus.at). In front are Otto Wagner's **Stadtbahn Pavilions** (Municipal Railway Pavilions), with their graceful green, gold and white motifs of sunflowers and tulips. Across the Kärntner Ring, the road becomes the Schubert and then the Park Ring as it passes the **Stadtpark**. The park is home to the famous gilded bronze and marble monument to Johann Strauss the Younger.

Applied Arts Museum

On the same side of the Ring, across Weiskirchnerstrasse is the **Museum für Angewandte Kunst** (Museum for Applied Arts; Wed–Sun 10am–6pm, Tue 10am–midnight; charge, Sat free; U-Bahn 3, tram 1, 2: Stubentor; U-Bahn 4: Landstrasse; www.mak.at). Known simply as MAK, this is one of the city's most exciting and thought-provoking museums. The exhibition rooms are designed by contemporary artists who often reveal unexpected other sides to quite mundane objects, such as the shadow play on Michael Thonet's bentwood chairs; you'll never view dining chairs in quite the same way again. There's a chance to see some particularly fine Viennese Biedermeier furnishings, as well as a collection of East Asian and Islamic art. The museum shop has a selection of items – design-conscious, arty and some downright humorous.

Biedermeier

The architecture, furniture and interior decoration known as 'Biedermeier' was produced in the period following Napoleon's defeat, between the Congress of Vienna in 1815 and the revolution in 1848. It was a time of political suppression in which the middle classes turned their attention to the arts. Biedermeier began as a satire, poking fun at the plodding German middle class. Two authors, Ludwig Eichrodt and Adolf Kussmaul, wrote poems in a journal called *Fliegende Blatter*, purporting to be the works of the unsophisticated 'Biedermeier', who, with his chum 'Bummelmeier', were boringly conventional. The name became synonymous with the age, but the work produced was far from dull. The Villa Wertheimstein *(see page 71)* and Dreimäderlhaus (Schreyvogelgasse 10) have fine examples of Biedermeier design; furniture is on display in the Museum for Applied Arts *(see above)*; and pieces can still be found in antiques shops.

Opposite the museum is Dr Karl Lueger-Platz. Here is the memorial to Dr Karl Lueger, the populist – and anti-Semitic – mayor of Vienna (1897–1910). The neighbouring **Café Pruckl** is a welcome sight if you need a break. The Stubenring passes near the **Postsparkasse** (Savings Bank), another masterpiece by Otto Wagner.

OUTSIDE THE RING

The Innere Stadt and the Ringstrasse by no means have a monopoly on sights. There's plenty more to be seen outside the Ring, from royal palaces to the Funeral Museum.

Hundertwasser Haus

Hundertwasser Haus facade

Dismissed by many as a bit of a joke, the whimsical **Hundertwasser Haus** is a hugely popular tourist attraction. This public housing complex in Kegelgasse was designed by Austria's best-known artist of recent times, Friedensreich Hundertwasser (1928–2000). The gently undulating facades of 52 apartments are decorated with bright paintwork, tiles, ceramics and onion domes. In the nearby Untere Weissgerberstrasse is Hundertwasser's own museum, the **Kunsthaus Wien** (daily 10am–7pm; charge; tram N, O: Radetzkyplatz; wheelchair

Incineration plant

Another of Friedensreich
Hundertwasser's projects
can be seen at the Fern-
wärmewerk at Spittelau
(U-Bahn: Spittelau; free
guided tours; www.wien
energie.at), an incinerator
whose output is used to
heat 60,000 homes. Deco-
rated by the artist in a
characteristically colourful
way, it is crowned by a vast
image of the artist's cap.

access; www.kunsthauswien.
com), which show both his
work and changing exhibi-
tions by his contemporaries.

Belvedere

The summer palace of Prince
Eugene of Savoy is regarded
as the finest flower of Vienna's baroque residential architecture. Though close to
the Innere Stadt, in the 3rd
District, the **Belvedere** (Unteres Belvedere, Thur–Tue
10am–6pm, Wed 10am–9pm; charge; Oberes Belvedere,
daily 10am–6pm; charge; tram D, 71; www.belvedere.at) is
an enchanted world apart with its allegorical sculptures,
fountains, waterfalls and gardens.

The **Unteres** (Lower) **Belvedere** was built by Johann
Lukas von Hildebrandt in 1714–16, and served as Prince Eugene's summer residence. (His winter palace is another jewel,
now brightening the lives of bureaucrats in the Finance Min-
istry on Himmelpfortgasse.) The palace was acquired by
Maria Theresa after the prince's death, and was used by various members of the Habsburg dynasty, including Archduke
Franz Ferdinand, whose assassination at Sarajevo in 1914
sparked off World War I. In 1955, the four victorious powers of World War II met in the Upper Belvedere to sign the
treaty for Austria's independence as a neutral country.

The Lower Belvedere was previously the location of the
collection of baroque art, but this has now moved to the
Oberes Belvedere and the space left is used for temporary exhibitions. Of the palace's wonderfully ornate interior the highlight is probably the highly ornate rococo gilt-and-mirrored

Golden Cabinet. The palace's **Orangerie** (access through the Lower Belvedere) was previously the Museum of Medieval Art, but the permanent collection has for the most part, like the baroque works, moved to the Oberes Belvedere. The Orangerie is now used to share the exhibitions put on in the rest of the palace. Beside the Orangerie is the **Prunkstall** (10am–midday), part of the stables and now used to display some more of the extensive holdings of medieval art previously hidden in the museum's depots.

Prince Eugene held banquets and other festivities in the **Oberes** (Upper) **Belvedere**, completed in 1723. Today it houses a wide-ranging **collection** of Austrian art from the Middle Ages to the present day. The gallery reflects the Austro-Hungarian Empire's image as a declining world power, culminating in a final grand artistic fling around 1900. As well as the excellent collections of medieval and baroque art (the

Prince Eugene's summer palace, the Lower Belvedere (1716)

latter including works by Franz Anton Maulbertsch and Martino Altomonte), there are fine examples of German Romanticism (including works by Caspar David Friedrich). However, the star exhibits for most people are from the collections of the *fin de siècle* and the Vienna Secession. These include such masterpieces as *The Kiss* by Gustav Klimt. Egon Schiele and Oskar Kokoschka are well represented. However, Klimt's portrait of *Adele Bloch-Bauer* no longer hangs in the gallery, as it was handed back to the Jewish family it had belonged to before the war (it was appropriated by the Nazis and had ended up in the Belvedere collection). The small but stunning collection of Impressionist and post-Impressionist art features works

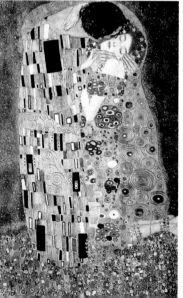

The Kiss by Gustav Klimt

by Monet, Renoir, Cézanne, Van Gogh and Munch, and sculptures by Rodin and Degas. The Upper Belvedere **terrace** offers a splendid view of the city skyline, remarkably little changed since Bellotto-Canaletto painted it in 1760. For your walk through the gardens, the best place to start is at the Oberes Belvedere. The sunset view is a pure delight.

Nearby Museums

Across Prinz-Eugene-Strasse from the Oberes Belvedere, at Goldeggasse 19, is the morbidly unique **Bestattungsmuseum** (Funeral Museum; Mon–Fri by appointment only; charge; tram D; www.

bestattungwien. at). At this typically Viennese institution you can learn all there is to learn about such devices as reusable coffins (after the ceremony, the hinged flaps would open and the corpse was left behind while the coffin was taken off to be used again). The museum's ashtrays are inscribed '*Rauchen sichert Arbeitsplätze*' ('Smoking Guarantees Jobs').

Close by in the Arsenal is the **Heeresgeschichtliches Museum** (Museum of Military History, daily 9am–5pm; charge; www.hgm.or.at). Housed in the earliest purpose-built museum in the city, the beautifully displayed, and extensive, holdings of the museum give a fascinating insight into the history of the Austrian state. The displays on World War II are hard-hitting, particularly the news footage of Vienna. One interesting, if slightly morbid, item on display is the blood-stained tunic of Archduke Franz Ferdinand.

Zentralfriedhof

The Viennese, it must be said, do not consider it morbid to be interested in funerals and admire *eine schöne Leich* (a nice corpse). They enjoy a walk through the **Zentralfriedhof** (Central Cemetery; Simmeringer Hauptstrasse 234; daily Nov–Feb 8am–5pm, Mar, Apr, Sept, Oct 7am–6pm, May–Aug 7am–7pm; tram 6, 71) in the southern district of Simmering. Opened in 1874, the cemetery has 200 hectares (500 acres) of funerary monuments that pay homage to the city's greats: musicians such as Beethoven, Schubert, Brahms and Schönberg, and writers Arthur Schnitzel and Franz Werfel. A map of the cemetery is available at Tor (Gate) 2.

The Gasometers

Also in Simmering are the **Gasometers** (U-Bahn 3: Gasometer; www.wiener-gasometer.at). These four gasholders were built for the city in 1896–9. Following their decommissioning in 1986, a scheme was launched to give the gasometers a new

lease of life. The complex opened in 2001 and it now contains shops, restaurants, cafés and bars, a multi-screen cinema and a hall seating 4,200 people. There are also offices, flats, student accommodation and the Vienna National Archives here.

Further Sights

To the west of the Ringstrasse, leading out from the MuseumsQuartier (see page 51), is **Mariahilferstrasse**, the city's most popular shopping street. Also, at No. 212, is the revamped **Technisches Museum** (Technical Museum; Mon–Fri 9am–6pm, Sat–Sun 10am–6pm; charge; tram

Gasometer interior

52, 58: Penzinger Strasse; www.technischesmuseum.at). The main hall has steam engines, a huge steel-making crucible and aeroplanes suspended above. There are wheels to turn and buttons to push, making this a great place for children, and the clearly laid-out exhibits explain the science behind many of the machines in an exemplary fashion.

Just to the south, along the Linke Wienzeile, are the fruit, vegetable and meat stalls of the famous **Naschmarkt** (food market), which has been here since the 16th century. Originally it was beside a river, the Wienfluss. In the 19th century the river was roofed over and stalls set up on the roof. Notice the decorated *Jugendstil* facade of **Majolikahaus** at No. 40, by Secessionist architect Otto Wagner. Nearby is the venerable

Theater an der Wien, built in 1801 for the impressario Emanuel Schikaneder, the librettist of Mozart's *Magic Flute*.

Further west is the **Haydnhaus** (Haydngasse 19; Tue–Sun 9am–6pm; charge; U-Bahn 3: Zieglergasse; www.wienmuseum.at). This is where the composer lived from 1797 until his death on 31 May 1809. His two oratorios *The Creation* and *The Seasons* were conceived and written in this house.

Further west still, in the suburb of Penzing (14th District), is one of Otto Wagner's most important works, the **Kirche am Steinhof** (guided tour only, Sat 3pm; charge; U-bahn 4 to Unter St Veit then bus 47A; www.wienkav.at). This masterpiece of *Jugendstil* design is the church for the Vienna's enlightened psychiatric hospital

North of the Innere Stadt, at Berggasse 19, is the **Freud Museum** (daily July–Sept 9am–6pm, Oct–June 9am–5pm; charge; tram D: Schlickgasse; www.freud-museum.at), dedicated to the father of psychoanalysis. Sigmund Freud lived here from 1891 until the arrival of the Nazis in 1938, when he fled to England. While most of his books and belongings are in London (including the couch), the waiting room has been faithfully reconstructed, with advice from his daughter Anna Freud. The entrance hall is particularly evocative, with his hat, walking stick and suitcase initialled SF. The rooms where he actually did his consulting now have a display on his life, while the rest of the apartment is given over to temporary exhibitions. One fascinating room has footage from home movies showing Freud during his final years.

Shopping at the Naschmarkt

Beyond the Freud Museum is the **Liechtenstein Museum** (Fri–Tue 10am–5pm; charge; tram D: Porzellangasse; www. lichtensteinmuseum.at), the garden palace of the princes of Liechtenstein. Now beautifully restored and showing off its wonderful frescoes, it holds an exceptionally fine collection of baroque paintings.

The **Schubert Geburtshaus** at Nussdorferstrasse 54 (Tue–Sun 10am–1pm, 2pm– 6pm; charge; tram 37, 38: Canisiusgasse; www.wienmuseum.at) is a museum set in the house where the composer was born in 1797.

SCHÖNBRUNN

Affairs of state were not something Maria Theresa shied away from, but she did prefer to handle them in the calmer setting of **Schönbrunn** (daily Nov–Mar 8.30am–4.30pm, Apr–June,

Schloss Schönbrunn, the imperial palace of Maria Theresa

Sept, Oct 8.30am–5pm, July, Aug 8.30am–6pm; charge; U-Bahn 4: Schönbrunn; tram 10, 58: Schönbrunn; bus 10A: Schönbrunn; www.schoen brunn.at). Almost as soon as she came to the throne in 1740, she moved into the palace, which Leopold I built as a summer residence and her father, Karl VI, had used as a shooting lodge. If the Hofburg is the oversized expression of a dynasty that outgrew itself, Schönbrunn is the smiling, serene expression

Schönbrunn garden walkway

of the personality of one woman, imperial nonetheless. Finding Fischer von Erlach's ideas for designing a 'super Versailles' too pompous, Maria Theresa brought in her favourite architect, Nikolaus Pacassi. He made Schönbrunn an imposing edifice, creating warm and decorative rococo interiors, which were a symbol of Maria Theresa's 'idyllic absolutism'.

The Gardens

To appreciate Schönbrunn's tendency to pleasure rather than imperial pomp, visit the **gardens** first. With the exception of the Kammergarten (Chamber Garden) and Kronprinzengarten (Crown Prince Garden) immediately left and right of the palace, the park has always been open to the public. Maria Theresa liked to have the Viennese around her. The park, laid out in classical French manner, is dominated by the **Gloriette,** a magnificent colonnade perched on the crest of a hill. It is difficult to say which view is prettier – the graceful silhouette of the Gloriette against a sunset viewed from the palace, or a bright morning view from the Gloriette over the whole of Vienna to the north and the Wienerwald away to the south.

On the way to the Gloriette you will pass the Neptune Fountain and countless other statues of ancient mythology. East of the fountain are the half-buried artificial **'Roman ruins'**, a romantic folly built by JF Hetzendorf von Hohenberg in 1778, complete with fragmented Corinthian columns, friezes and archways. Nearby is the Schöner Brunnen, the 'beautiful spring' discovered by Emperor Matthias around 1615, from which the palace took its name and which provided the water supply. West of Neptune is the **Tiergarten** (zoo), established in 1752 by François of Lorraine, the consort of Maria Theresa. Not everyone enjoys seeing animals behind bars, but the aquarium, with its 'walk-through' flooded rainforest, is worth a visit. You can also lose yourself in the topiary **maze** and a **Tyrolean Garden**. Other attractions include the **Palmenhaus** (Palm House) and **Wüstenhaus** (Desert Experience House).

Schönbrunn sculpture

The Palace

Crossing the courtyard to the palace's front entrance, you'll see on the right the **Schlosstheater**, now the site of summer chamber-opera performances.

A conducted tour of the **palace** reveals something of the cosy ambience enjoyed by Maria Theresa and her successors: her breakfast room, decorated with the needlework of the empress and her myriad daughters; the **Spiegelsaal** (Hall of Mirrors), in which the young Mozart gave his first royal recital; the **Chinesisches Rundkabinett** (Chinese Round Room), also known as Maria Theresa's Konspirationstafelstube ('Top Secret Dining Room'). For her secret consultations, a table rose from the floor with a completely prepared dinner so that no servants would be present during the conversation. Guests used the **billiard room** while awaiting an audience with Franz Joseph. He, too, preferred Schönbrunn to the Hofburg and kept his mistress, actress Katharina Schratt, in a villa in the neighbouring district of Hietzing. Also on view is the bedroom where he died on 30 November 1916, at the age of 86.

The stately and the human are poignantly juxtaposed in the opulence of the ballrooms and dining rooms and the intimacy of the living quarters. The **Napoleon Room** (originally Maria Theresa's bedroom) was used by the French emperor on his way to victory at Austerlitz and by his son, the Duke of Reichstadt, in his final sad years. It is both pathetic and awesome to sense Napoleon's presence in a room that now contains his son's death mask and stuffed pet bird. Down the corridor, the last Habsburg abdicated at the end

Flash fittings

The most ornate room at Schönbrunn is known as the MillionsRoom, with walls panelled in costly rosewood in the rococo style. Gilt-edged cartouches set into wood contain Indian miniature paintings showing the court and private lives of the 16th- and 17th-century Moghul emperors. To make them fit, original paintings were cut up by members of the imperial family and arranged as collages to form new pictures.

of World War I and Kennedy and Khrushchev met for dinner at the height of the Cold War. In the adjoining **Wagenburg Museum** (Apr–Oct daily 9am–6pm, Nov–Mar Tue–Sun 10am–4pm; charge; www.khm.at) you can see an impressive collection of coaches used by the imperial court, including the gilded coronation car of Karl VI.

ACROSS THE DANUBE

The Prater

Over the Aspernbrücke, cross the Donaukanal at the junction of Franz-Josefs-Kai and Stubenring to reach the island between the Donaukanal and the much wider main channel to the east. The southern part is occupied by the **Prater** (15 Mar–31 Oct daily 10am–midnight; www.praterservice.at). This is Vienna's most extensive park, once reserved for the nobility but opened up to the public in 1766 by Emperor Joseph II. Its most prominent feature is the old-fashioned amusement park with the famous **Riesenrad** (Ferris Wheel; Jan–Feb 10am– 7.45pm, Mar–Apr 10am–9.45pm, Apr–Sept 9am– 11.45pm; charge; www.wienerriesenrad.com) that was

The Riesenrad at the Prater

immortalised in the film *The Third Man*. Built in 1897, it is one of the oldest and largest Ferris wheels in the world, 65m (213ft) high, and provides a great view over the city. Next to the Riesenrad is the terminal of the **Liliput-Bahn** (Lilliput Railway; www.liliputbahn.com), which on summer weekends provides transport around the park.

Donauinsel

You can reach the real Danube River (as opposed to the Danube Canal) along Lassallestrasse and over the Reichsbrücke. An artificial recreation island featuring beaches, barbecue picnic areas and sports facilities, the **Donauinsel** runs 21km (13 miles) along the middle of the river. The 'Blue Danube' is actually yellowish-brown in colour due to the lime content of the riverbed. Continue on the Wagramerstrasse, past the attractive modern complex of buildings forming the **UNO-City** (officially the Vienna International Centre; guided tours

The soaring Millennium Tower

Mon–Fri 11am, 2pm; bring your passport; www.unvienna. org) to the **Alte Donau** (the Old Danube). This self-contained arm of the river is closed off for sailing, fishing and bathing, and is blue. The banks are lined with beaches, marinas and neat gardens.

The **Donaupark** links the old and new Danube. More tranquil than the Prater, it has been laid out with flower beds, an artificial lake and sports arenas. It also features the 252m (827ft) tall **Donauturm** (Danube Tower), with fine views from its terrace. Back on the city side of the Danube, at Handelskai near the Nordbahnbrücke, is the **Millennium Tower**, completed in 1999. At over 200m (656ft), this is the tallest enclosed building in Central Europe.

Vienna viewed from the vineyards of Kahlenberg

VIENNA'S SUBURBS

You should devote at least a day to exploring the 19th District of **Döbling**, the most gracious and elegant of Vienna's suburbs. Stretching from the Danube Canal to the slopes of the Wienerwald, Döbling includes Sievering, Grinzing, Heiligenstadt, Nussdorf and Kahlenberg. It is dotted with villas, parks, vineyards and, of course, the *Heuriger* wine gardens, which are especially popular in **Grinzing**.

Heiligenstadt and the other neighbourhoods of Döbling provide a vital clue to the secret of Vienna's charm. Vienna is not a conventional big city, but rather a collection of villages clustered around the Innere Stadt. These village-suburbs provide a convenient getaway from what the Viennese call the *Hektik* of metropolitan life.

Catch tram 37 in front of the Votivkirche at Schottentor (or take U-bahn 4 to its terminus), and take it to **Heiligenstadt**, the heart of Vienna's 'Beethoven country'. You may want to stop off en route at the **Eroica Haus** (Döblinger Hauptstrasse 92; Fri 3–6pm; charge; www.wienmuseum.at), where Beethoven worked on his *Eroica* symphony during 1803–4, and at **Villa Wertheimstein** (Döblinger Hauptstrasse 96), a masterpiece of 19th-century Biedermeier architecture, full of period pieces, and featuring a lovely English garden.

At the end of the line (Heiligenstädter Park), walk across the park past the monument to Beethoven to Pfarrplatz 2, the prettiest of the composer's many Viennese homes. Take bus 38A to Probusgasse 6, the house where, in 1802, the composer penned his tragic *Heiligenstadt Testament*, in which he told his two brothers of his encroaching deafness. Today it is the **Beethoven Wohnung Heiligenstadt** (Tue–Sun 10am–1pm and 2–6pm; charge; www.wienmuseum.at).

The Hohenstrasse

To explore the hills and woods that lie to the north of the city, take the 38A bus from Heiligenstadt U-bahn up to the **Höhenstrasse** leading to Kahlenberg and Leopoldsberg on the northern slopes of the Wienerwald. The route offers a grandiose view of the city and surrounding country. You'll find it difficult to believe that you're still inside the city limits. If time permits, get out at one of the stops en route and have a walk around.

Near the end of the Hohenstrasse is the **Kahlenberg**. Since the end of the 18th century, the heights of Kahlenberg have been dotted with fashionable summer homes offering what is known as *Sommerfrische* (cool summer respite from the city heat). During two steaming hot days in July 1809, the Viennese aristocracy had a grandstand view of Napoleon's Battle of Wagram against the Austrians. Sipping cool Nussdorfer white wine, they watched the slaughter of 40,000 Austrians and 34,000 Frenchmen on the other side of the Danube.

The Höhenstrasse goes as far as **Leopoldsberg**, the very edge of the Wienerwald and the extreme eastern point of the European Alps. On a clear day, you can see about 100km (60 miles) eastwards from the terrace of the **Leopoldskirche** to the Carpathian Mountains of Slovakia.

Klosterneuburg

A short detour 7km (4 miles) to the north takes you to the imposing Augustine abbey of **Klosterneuburg** (daily 9am–6pm; charge; U-bahn 4 to Heiligenstadt and then bus 237, 238 or 239; www.stift-klosterneuburg.at). A story claims it was founded by Duke Leopold III of Babenberg in 1106 on

Klosterneuburg abbey

the spot where his bride's lost veil was discovered by his hunting dogs. In fact, its foundation is earlier, but little of the original edifice remains. Karl VI, who was very much taken with Spain, undertook major alterations in the 18th century, making it a baroque version of El Escorial. He wanted a combined palace and church with nine domes, each topped with a crown of the House of Habsburg. Only two were completed in his lifetime: the crown of the empire on the big dome and of the Austrian archduchy on the little one.

Klosterneuburg also features a museum of modern

art, the **Essl Museum** (Tue, Thur–Sun 10am–6pm, Wed 10am–9pm; charge; free shuttle from Operngasse 4; www. sammlung-essl.at), a private foundation devoted to avant-garde Austrian artists and some of their American and European contemporaries.

The baroque ornamentation is indeed impressive, but the whole trip is made worthwhile by the **Leopoldskapelle**, with its magnificent **Verdun Altar** of 1181 containing 45 enamelled panels depicting scenes from the Scriptures. It served as a graphic Bible for the poor who could not read the stories.

Escaping the city

The sights around Vienna, from the Wienerwald to further afield in Burgenland, are all easily reached as a day trip from the city, using Austria's excellent network of public transport. The train (see www.oebb.at) will get you to most places, and those sights without a station will be served by connecting buses (see www.postbus.at).

THE WIENERWALD

While it can be seen along the Höhenstrasse, to appreciate the **Wienerwald** properly, you must visit the villages hidden away in the forest to the south and southwest of Vienna (for information on local buses and trains check on www.wiener linien.at). First head out to Perchtoldsdorf, a serene little village amid heather-covered hills, vineyards and fir trees. Continue south to Burg Liechtenstein, a 'ruined castle' built in 1873 on the site of the 12th-century home of the Liechtenstein dynasty. The park is an ideal spot for a picnic. In **Mödling** you can see the 15th-century Gothic Spitalkirche (Hospital Church) and the house (Hauptstrasse 79) where Beethoven worked on his *Missa Solemnis*.

To the west is **Hinterbrühl**. Romantics like to believe that the picturesque mill, Höldrichsmühle (converted into an inn), is where Franz Schubert wrote songs for the miller's daughter Rosi ('*Die schöne Müllerin*') in 1823. In fact the story originated in an 1864 operetta devoted to the composer's life. But the inn's wines can make believers of us all.

Beyond is the Sattelbach Valley and the Cistercian abbey of **Heiligenkreuz** (Holy Cross), founded in 1133. Heiligenkreuz is named after the relic of a piece of the True Cross, given to Austria by the King of Jerusalem in the 12th century and kept in the tabernacle behind the high altar. The courtyard features a **Trinity Column** (Pillar of the Plague), the work of baroque artist Giovanni Giuliani, who also designed the basilica's splendid choir stalls. The structure retains its Romanesque western facade. Along its south side is a graceful 13th-century cloister with 300 red columns.

In the town **churchyard** you'll find a tomb bearing the inscription: '*Wie eine Blume sprosst der Mensch auf und wird gebrochen*' ('Like a flower, the human being unfolds – and is broken'). This is the grave of Baroness Mary Vetsera, the 17-year-old who died in 1889 at nearby **Mayerling** in an apparent suicide pact with her lover Crown Prince Rudolf, heir to the Austro-Hungarian Empire. To hush the scandalmongers, the hunting lodge where the Mayerling tragedy occurred was demolished shortly thereafter and replaced with a Carmelite convent.

Baden

From town the Badner Bahn (www.wlb.at) will take you from the Kärntner Ring to the romantic Helenental Valley and the spa of **Baden bei Wien**, 25km (16 miles) south of Vienna. Enjoyed by the Romans and made fashionable by Franz I in 1803, Baden became the very symbol of upright Viennese Biedermeier prosperity. The gentry of Vienna built their summer villas here and bathed in the 36°C (97°F) sulphurous waters. The thermal waters can still be enjoyed in the indoor pool (Brusattiplatz 4), open-air pools (Helenen Strasse 19–21) and mineral-water pools (Marchetti Strasse 13). Return via **Gumpoldskirchen**, a village with first-rate *Heuriger* wine gardens and not a bad place to stay if you want to be out of town (see page 133).

THE DANUBE VALLEY

If your visit gives you time for only one side-trip it should unquestionably be along the **Danube Valley**, in particular the magical area known as the Wachau between the historic towns of Melk and Krems. About an hour west of Vienna, this is where the Danube Valley is at its most scenic – by turns both charming and smiling with vineyards, apricot orchards and rustic villages, then suddenly forbidding with ruined medieval castles and rocky cliffs half hidden in mist.

The ruined 13th-century Burg Aggstein

This is a landscape whose atmosphere is heavy with myth. Legend has it that the Burgundy kings of the medieval German epic, the *Nibelungenlied*, passed this spot en route to the kingdom of the Huns. The crusaders also passed through here on their way to the Holy Land. Take the Danube River Steamer if you simply want to sit and dream as this mythical world passes you by. For a closer look at the towns and castles on the way it's best to travel around by train or bus.

Melk

On a leisurely tour of the Danube Valley, 84km (52 miles) by the Westautobahn from Vienna, the Benedictine abbey of **Melk**

The abbey of Melk

(Stift Melk; daily Apr–Oct 9am–5.30pm, Nov–Mar only by guided tour 11am, 2pm; charge; www. stiftmelk.at) makes an ideal starting point. Towering high above the river on a protruding rock, this is one of the region's most majestic sights. Its position overlooking a bend in the river made this a strategic site from the time of the Romans. The Babenberg predecessors of the Habsburgs had a palace stronghold here in the 10th century, which they handed over to the Benedictines in 1106. The monks gradually created an abbey of huge proportions, enhanced by the baroque transformations of architect Jakob

Prandtauer in 1702. Two towers, together with the octagonal dome and the lower Bibliothek (Library) and Marmorsaal (Marble Hall), form a harmonious group. The interior of the church is rich in reds and golds with a high altar by Antonio Beduzzi and superbly sculpted pulpit, choir and confessionals. The ceiling frescoes are by Johann Michael Rottmayr, whose work also adorns Vienna's Karlskirche.

Before crossing the Danube, make a quick detour to the village of **Mauer**, 10km (6 miles) due east of Melk, to see the late Gothic wooden altarpiece in the parish church. The work, by an anonymous local artist around 1515, depicts the *Adoration of the Virgin Mary* with a wealth of vivid detail.

Medieval Towns of the Wachau

The Wachauer Strasse, along the north bank, is dotted with apricot orchards and vineyards, old *Weinhüterhütten* (vineguards' huts) and villages with *Heuriger* wine gardens.

On the opposite bank, you can see Schönbühel and the 13th-century ruins of **Burg Aggstein**. The castle was once owned by a robber baron named Jörg Scheck vom Wald, popularly known as 'Schreckenwald' (Terror of the Forest). One of his favourite activities was to lead prisoners to his rose garden, on the edge of a sheer precipice, where they were given the choice of either starving to death or ending it quickly by jumping 53m (175ft) onto the rocks below.

Back on the happier north bank, visit the town of **Spitz**, with its late Gothic **St Mauritius** church. It's known for its statues of the Apostles in the 1380 organ gallery, and the baroque painting of the *Martyrdom of St Mauritius* by Kremser (Martin Johann) Schmidt. In the village of **St Michael**, look for seven stone hares perched on the roof of the 16th-century church. These commemorate a particularly vicious winter when snowdrifts were said to have enabled the animals to jump clear over the church. In the village of

Weissenkirchen is a fortified church, which was originally surrounded by four towers, a moat, ramparts and 44 cannons.

The most romantic of these medieval towns is **Dürnstein**, famous as the site of Richard the Lion Heart's imprisonment in 1192–3. Devastated by the Swedish army in 1645, the castle of Kuenringer is more interesting to look at from below than it is to visit. But do make a point of seeing Dürnstein's **abbey church**, a baroque structure with a splendid carved wooden door to the abbey courtyard and an imposing statue of the resurrected Christ at the church entrance.

Krems

Krems is the heart of the region's wine industry and historically one of the Danube Valley's most important trading centres. Today, you can enjoy its superb Gothic, Renaissance and baroque residences on tranquil, tree-shaded squares. Start on Südtiroler Platz and walk through the 15th-century Steiner Tor (Town Gate) with its Gothic pepper-pot towers. Turn left up Schmidgasse to Körnermarkt and the Dominikanerkirche

A Song for Richard

During the Crusade of 1191, the brave but cheeky English king, Richard the Lion Heart, enraged Leopold V von Babenberg by replacing the Austrian flag in Acre, Palestine, with the English one. Worse than that, he prevented the Austrians from sharing in the booty. But, on his way home, though dressed as a peasant, Richard was recognised and thrown into the darkest dungeon of Dürnstein. He languished there for several years until the faithful minstrel Blondel came looking for him, singing a song known only to the king and himself. Richard revealed his place of imprisonment by joining in the chorus. His ransom, 23,000kg (22.6 tons) of silver, was enough to finance the Holy Roman Empire's expedition to Sicily and to build a new Ring Wall around Vienna.

Prosperous Krems

(Dominican Church), transformed into an important museum of medieval art. Continue round to Pfarrplatz, dominated by the **Pfarrkirche**, a lovely church remodelled (1616–30) by two Italian architects and decorated with altar paintings by Franz Anton Maulbertsch and the masterful frescoes of Kremser Schmidt. The oldest square in Krems, Hoher Markt, features a masterpiece of Gothic residential architecture, the arcaded **Gozzoburg**, built around 1270. Take a stroll along the Untere Landstrasse to see some elegant baroque facades and the fine Renaissance **Rathaus** (Town Hall). On a contemporary note, a modern art museum has opened in the town, the **Kunsthalle Krems** (www.kunsthalle.at) and close by a **Karikaturmuseum** (www.karikaturmuseum.at). It includes work by the Austrian cartoonist Manfred Deix, who was renowned for being less than flattering to his fellow-countrymen.

Before leaving Krems, try some of the local 'new wine' served in one of the leafy courtyards along the Obere Landstrasse.

TO THE EAST

Heading east from Vienna along the Danube traces the ancient eastern European boundary of the Roman Empire. About 36km (22 miles) from the city, at Petronell, are the remains of **Carnuntum**, which was once the capital of the Roman province of Pannonia (embracing much of modern Hungary and eastern Austria). In the 2nd century AD, under Hadrian and Marcus Aurelius, it was a thriving commercial centre. A summer festival is held in the Roman amphitheatre.

Five kilomtres (3 miles) south of Petronell is **Rohrau**, the birthplace of Joseph Haydn. You can visit the beautifully restored thatched farmhouse where he was born in 1732. Concerts are held here during spring and summer. Nearby is the Schloss Rohrau, the baroque castle of the Harrach family, early patrons of young Haydn. The castle has a fine collection of 17th-century Spanish, Flemish and Italian art.

Neusiedlersee

Beyond Rohrau, and further east, is the **Neusiedler See**. This birdwatchers' paradise teems with heron, teal, waterfowl, wild geese and egret. The water of the lake is so shallow that it's possible to wade right across – only a few spots are more than 1.5m (5ft) deep. If you do cross, make sure you're armed with your passport for your arrival on the other side – the southern end of the lake belongs to Hungary. Flat-bottomed boats can be hired for fishing. In winter

Fishermen at Neusiedlersee

you can go skating and ice-sailing. Along the lake's western shores are the villages of **Rust** and **Mörbisch**. Both are famous for the storks that favour their chimneys for nesting. Mörbisch, on the Hungarian border, is particularly attractive, and the wine gardens are idyllic.

Stork nesting in Rust

Eisenstadt

The baroque town of **Eisenstadt**, 52km (32 miles) south of Vienna, is where Joseph Haydn worked from 1761 as musical director for the Hungarian prince Paul Esterházy. His house, the **Haydn-Haus** (Apr–Oct daily 9am–5pm; charge; www.haydnhaus.at), contains his collection of paintings, sheets of music and personal possessions. Haydn loved Eisenstadt and wanted to live and die here. He managed the living, but died in Vienna, without having taken the precaution of specifying where he wanted to be buried. Unfortunately, shortly after he was buried in Vienna in 1809, someone stole his skull, which was put on exhibition. The headless body was eventually returned to Eisenstadt where the skull rejoined it in 1954. He is now in a white marble grave at the **Bergenkirche**. The church is also noted for a Kalvarienberg, a Calvary display of life-size figures showing the stations of the cross, displayed in a series of austere dungeon-like rooms.

WHAT TO DO

ENTERTAINMENT

Opera

Its difficult to think of a cultural institution in another European capital that holds the privileged place of the **Staatsoper** (National Opera; www.weiner-staatsoper.at) in Vienna. Since this is Austria, even people who loathe opera (never having seen one) can be tempted in and converted. Try to make Mozart your first opera; after that you'll be ready to take on Wagner and even Alban Berg.

If you have tickets for a première or other gala performance, you should wear evening dress, though even on an ordinary night, people turn up in black tie or long dress.

First-rate opera and operetta can also be heard at the **Volksoper** (Währingerstrasse 78; www.volksoper.at), and opera and ballet at the **Theater an der Wien** (Linke Wienzeile 6; www.theater-wien.at).

Music

Music is an integral part of Vienna. There really is something for everyone, with concerts held in historic buildings, including Schönbrunn and the Belvedere. However, the really serious music-making takes place in the city's famous concert halls, chief amongst them the **Musikverein** (Dumbastrasse 3; www.musikverein.at), now with four new halls. The other major hall is the **Konzerthaus** (Lothringerstrasse 20; www.konzerthaus.at).

Festivals take place throughout the year, the most important being the **Wiener Festwochen** (www.festwochen.at). The festivals and concert seasons are showcases for the city's ensembles, including the **Wiener Philharmoniker** (www.

wienerphilharmoniker.at), one of the world's finest orchestras. Other fine orchestras resident in the city include the **Wiener Symphoniker** (www.wiener-symphoniker.at), and the **Radio Symphonie Orchester Wien** (www.rso.orf.at). **Klang Forum Wien** (www.klangforum.at) specialises in contemporary music, while the **Concentus Musicus Wien** (www.concentus-musicus.com) is one of Europe's most important early-music ensembles.

Of course, there are many opportunities to hear the music of composers associated with the city. In fact, the music of Mozart, Haydn, Schubert and Beethoven is performed in Vienna's oldest concert hall, the **Sala Terrena** (Singerstrasse 7; www.mozarthaus.at). You should also try to hear the celebrated **Wiener Sängerknaben** (Vienna Boys' Choir), who sing at Sunday Mass and other festivities in the Burgkapelle in the Hofburg *(see page 45)*.

Performance in the Musikverein

Theatre

The **Burgtheater** (National Theatre; Dr-Karl-Lueger-Ring 2; www.burgtheater. at) is not just Vienna's proudest theatre, but also one of the leading ensembles of the German-speaking world. The related **Akademietheater** (Lisztrasse 1) focuses on modern and avant-garde drama.

Performances are held all year round at Vienna's **English Theatre** at Josefsgasse 12 (www.englishtheatre.at). There are several English-speaking theatre groups in the city, and special performances are staged for children. Not far from here is the excellent **Josefstadt Theater** (Josefstädter Strasse 26; www.josefstadt.org) that always has interesting productions.

Cinema

Austrian cinema has a long history, stretching back to the early years of silent film. Vienna itself has some excellent cinemas, including the newly renovated **Filmmuseum** (www. filmmuseum.at), underneath the Albertina, that puts on screenings of classic European- and English-language films. The **Burg Kino** on the Ringstrasse (www.burgkino.at) shows original-language English movies, as well as regular screenings of *The Third Man* (currently on Fridays at 10.45pm).

Elsewhere, the **Urania Kino** in the observatory at the end of the Stubenring (Uraniastrasse 1) has a nice auditorium, while the **Künstlerhaus Kino** (www.k-haus.at) on Karlsplatz is the place to catch avant-garde and art-house films, as well as being the venue for a number of film festivals.

Nightlife

The city is said to have more than 6,000 bars, nightclubs, discos and cabarets – with many of the most popular

Listings

Clubs come and go, so consult a copy of *Falter*, the weekly listings magazine, for the latest information about nightclubs, parties and lounges.

Bar stools

bars staying open round the clock. There are a few large clubs, but also many small venues with music provided by well-known DJs. There are cool lounge clubs, too, where people chill out to easy-listening sounds.

North of Stephansdom, the area around Ruprechtsplatz, Seitenstettengasse and Rabensteig forms the previously hot **Bermudadreieck** (Bermuda Triangle). Apart from the excellent **First Floor** bar (Seitenstettengasse 5), this area is now passé, and much of the action has passed on to the district around Naschmarkt and the railway arches along the **Hernalser Gürtel** (on the western edge of the 8th District). The district around **Bäckerstrasse** is also chic. The tacky nightclubs around **Kärntnerstrasse** cater largely to the tourist trade.

Over on the Donaukanal is one of Vienna's best-known clubs, **Flex** (www.flex.at), with a legendary sound system and top DJs as well as live bands. Other popular places include **Passage** (www.sunshine.at), literally under the Burgring and formed out of a converted underpass; and, in the 12th District, **U4** (www.u-4.at), a long-standing club and live music venue. Along the Gürtel the scene revolves around chic bars with DJs and some live music. Good places to check out include **Chelsea** (www.chelsea.co.at), occupying a converted railway arch and known for its pulsating live music; the hardcore electronic venue of **rhiz** (www.rhiz.org); and the more chic and laid-back **Q[kju:]** (www.kju-bar.at).

SHOPPING

Perhaps surprisingly, Vienna has a lot to offer for those keen to go shopping. Behind many of the city's grand facades – or at least those spaces that have not been snapped up by international chains – are quirky boutiques, elegant design shops or long-standing purveyors of luxury handmade goods, from shoes and *Tracht*, to cakes and pastries.

Where and When to Shop

The winding streets of Vienna's **Inner City** are a good place to start any shopping expedition. Although now increasingly dominated by international names, especially along **Graben**, **Kohlmarkt** and **Kärntnerstrasse**, there are still numerous interesting local places to ferret out. To the west of the Inner City, **Mariahilferstrasse** is the other main shopping area: a long series of shops which only peters out at the Westbahnhof. Other good shopping districts can be found in the **university district** (near the Votivkirche) and around **Siebensterngasse** and **Lindengasse** in Neubau (the 7th District). Shops tend to be open between 9am and 6pm on weekdays, closing at 5pm on Saturday. Most places remain shut on Sundays.

Shoppers on the Graben

What to Buy

For general fashion a good place to start is **Steffl**, a large department store (Kärntnerstrasse 19) with a large number of concessions for both well-established and younger designers. Otherwise have a wander through the **Ringstrassen Galerien** nearby on the Kärtner Ring. In the 1st District most of the big name designers can be found around Kohlmarkt with some of the more interesting stuff to be found at the very funky **2006FEB01** (Plankengasse 3) or the offshoot from long-standing Austrian hat-makers Mühlbauer at **Mode** (Seilergasse 5). Further afield check out the boutiques on Lindengasse and for up-and-coming Austrian designers do not miss **PARK** on Mondscheingasse (No. 20) close by.

For beautifully made *Tracht* (traditional Austrian clothing still popular in Vienna), go to **Tostmann Trachten** (Schottengasse 31) or **Loden-Plankl** (Michaelerplatz 6).

Dried fruit at the Naschmarkt

Vienna can also boast two world-class shoe makers. Neither **Rudolf Scheer** (Bräunerstrasse 4) or **Ludwig Reiter** (Mölkersteig 1) are cheap but their shoes are superbly crafted.

Classic Viennese designs are other items worth seeking out. For glass and porcelain head for **Augarten** (Stock-im-Eisen Platz 3) and **Lobmeyer** (Kärntnerstrasse 26). Wiener Werkstätte textiles can be found at **Backhausen** (Schwarzenbergstrasse 10) who also have a museum of

Christmas market
at the Rathaus

original works in the basement of the shop. For replicas of classic lamps and lighting check out **Woka** (Palais Breuner, Singerstrasse 16). Good examples of contemporary Austrian design can be found at **artup** (Bauernmarkt 8).

As such an important centre for classical music Vienna has a couple of excellent places to buy CDs and sheet music. **Gramola** (Graben 16 and Seilerstätte 30, below the Haus der Musik) is the best place to find recordings, while **Doblinger** (Dorotheergasse 10) has a vast selection of scores.

For food and drink head for the city's best market on **Naschmarkt** or the wonderful selection at **Julius Meinl** (Kohlmarkt 1). Seasonal specialities can be found in the Christmas markets that take place outside the Rathaus or the Spittelberg district. Wonderful patisserie can be found at confectioners such as **Demel** (Kohlmarkt 14) and **Gerstner** (Kärntnerstrasse 13), with what is claimed to be the original *Sachertorte* on sale at the **Sacher** (Philharmonikerstrasse 4).

ACTIVE PURSUITS

The easiest way to get rid of excess *strudel* is by going for a walk or run in one of the city's many **parks**. The largest of these is the Prater , but there are parks dotted all around the Ringstrasse that give you a chance to stretch your legs.

Cycling is an enjoyable way of getting around Vienna – and of escaping traffic snarls. Bicycles can be rented from any one of 160 Austrian railway stations. In Vienna, the three stations that rent bicycles are Westbahnhof, Wien Nord and Floridsdorf. You can return your bicycle to any participating Austrian railway station. The free *See Vienna by Bike* brochure from the Tourist Information Office lists bicycle hire firms, and also provides regional maps of cycling routes. See Vienna's spectacular hinterland by **hiking** along the well-marked paths of the Wienerwald. In the winter, these paths can be used for **cross-country skiing**.

The 21km (13-mile) beach of the Donauinsel *(see page 69)* provides outdoor **swimming**, along with facilities for **waterskiing** and **windsurfing**. Döbling's **Krapfenwaldlbad** is a fashionable outdoor swimming pool, complete with champagne bar. Most handsome of the indoor swimming pools is the **Amalienbad**, Reumannplatz 23, with *Jugendstil* decor and an old-fashioned steam bath and sauna.

Ice-skating carries on year-round in the Wiener Stadthalle, Vogelweidplatz 14, and during the winter in Rathausplatz outside the town hall.

You can see professional football in the Prater, home of one the city's first division teams, Austria Vienna.

Youth centre

For information about events and activities for young people (aged 13 to 26), contact Jugendinfo at Babenbergerstrasse 1 (Mon–Sat noon–7pm, tel: 1799; www. jugendinfo-wien.at).

CHILDREN'S VIENNA

Vienna is a good destination for children. **Schönbrunn** *(see page 64)* has a number of distractions: there is the **Marionette Theatre** and maze, and a cellar devoted to the baking and tasting of *strudel*. There's also a **zoo** at Schönbrunn and a **vivarium** at Esterhazy Park. Also try the **Butterfly House** at Burggarten, and, for those who like stars, the city's **Planetarium** (Oswald Thomas Platz; www.planetarium-wien.at). Outside the city, on the eastern slopes of the Wienerwald, the **Lainz Wildlife Park** offers carriage rides, forest playgrounds, nature trails and even close-up encounters with wild boar.

The **ZOOM Kindermuseum** *(see page 52)* is specifically for children, while the **Museum of Modern Art Ludwig Foundation**, **Museum of Fine Arts** and **Museum of Natural History** all have children's programmes, and the **Technical Museum** and the **House of Music** both have lots to discover.

The **Prater funfair**, the **Spanish Riding School** *(see page 42)* and the view from the **Donauturm** *(see page 69)* are all must-sees. Playgrounds and beaches can be found on **Danube Island**. In summer, the **boats** on the Danube sometimes have children's events (www.ddsg-bluedanube.at).

Kids at Schönbrunn

Calendar of Events

For information and ticket details, contact the Tourist Information Office, tel: 2111 4222, or consult www.info.wien.at.

January Vienna Philharmonic's traditional *Neujahrskonzert* (New Year's Day concert), 11am at Musikverein; jazz-lovers' alternative: Vienna Art Orchestra, 9pm at Sofiensäle, Marxergasse 17.

February/March *Opernball* (Opera Ball), at Staatsoper, the social event of the year; the *Ball der Philharmoniker* (Philharmonic Ball), at Musikverein, rivals the *Opernball* for prestige; *Fasching* (Carnival) procession in Döbling.

April *Ostermarkt* (Easter Market): a country-fair atmosphere on Freyung in Innere Stadt; *Wiener Sängerknaben* (Vienna Boys' Choir) weekly Mass in the Hofburg's Burgkapelle; *OsterKlang Wien* (Vienna's Sounds of Easter) music festival.

May Traditional May Day celebrations at Prater amusement park; Vienna Marathon accompanied by popular festivities; the Life Ball, an AIDS charity event supported by international celebrities.

June *Wiener Festwochen* (Vienna Festival), featuring music, dance and theatrical productions at Theater an der Wien and Messepalast; Regenbogen (Gay Rainbow) Parade on Ringstrasse; *Donaueninselfest* (Danube Island Festival), with funfair festivities.

July/August *Jazzfest Wien* (Vienna Jazz Festival) at Staatsoper and Burgtheater; Donauinsel pop music festival, a free weekend event; *Wiener Musiksommer*, summer festival of popular opera and operetta at Theater an der Wien; *Klangbogen* musical recitals in palaces and outdoors; jazz, rock, reggae and hip-hop music festival at Wiesen, south of Vienna.

September Schönbrunn Palace festival; In-line Skating Marathon on the Ringstrasse.

October Viennale Film Festival; *Wean Hean* folk festival.

November/December *Christkindlmarkt* (Christmas Market) at Rathausplatz, Schönbrunn, Freyung, Spittelberg: carols, roast chestnuts, *Glühwein* and stalls laden with gifts; MuseumsQuartier courtyard decked with lights and decorations; concerts, recitals throughout the Innere Stadt; New Year's Eve *Kaiserball* (Emperor's Ball) opens the ball season in Hofburg.

EATING OUT

When it comes to Viennese cuisine, it is worth bearing in mind that this city was once the centre of the old Habsburg Empire of 60 million Eastern and Southern Europeans. The emperor and his archdukes and generals have gone, but not the Bohemian dumplings, the Hungarian goulash, the Polish stuffed cabbage and Serbian *schaschlik*, and the plum, cherry and apricot brandies that accompany the Turkish coffee. And all are now frequently served with the lighter touch of the New Viennese Cuisine.

Sautéed to perfection, *Wienerschnitzel* as served at Figlmüller

VIENNESE FARE

Two Viennese staples that you're likely to come across immediately are the *Wienerschnitzel* and the *Backhendl*. The *Wienerschnitzel* is a large, thinly sliced cutlet of veal crisply sautéed in a coating of egg and seasoned breadcrumbs. *Backhendl* is roast chicken prepared in the same way. Viennese gourmets insist that the *Wienerschnitzel* be served with cold potato or cucumber salad. You should also make sure that it is a cut of veal *(vom Kalb)* and not pork *(vom Schwein)*, as in some of the cheaper establishments. The *Backhendl* is sometimes served with *Geröstete* (sautéed potatoes).

Tafelspitz (boiled beef) was Emperor Franz Joseph's favourite dish, and to this day is a form of ambrosia to the Viennese. Spice it up with *Kren* (horseradish) and *Schnitt-lauchsauce* (chive sauce). Another delight, originally from Hungary, is goulash – beef chunks stewed in onions, garlic, paprika, tomatoes and celery. *Debreziner* sausages, *Kömény-magleves Nokedival* (caraway-seed soup with dumplings) and apple soup are three more Hungarian specialities.

From the Czech Republic comes Prague ham and *sauer-kraut* soup; from Polish Galicia, roast goose; and from Ser-bia, peppery barbecued *cevapcici* meatballs and *schaschlik* brochettes of lamb with onions and green and red peppers.

Dumplings *(Knödel)*, made from flour, yeast or potatoes, are an Austrian staple. The *Marillenknödel* is a dessert dumpling, made of potato with a piping hot apricot inside. Another delicious dessert dumpling is the *Topfenknödel*, made with a cream-cheese filling.

Hot desserts are, in fact, a speciality, and you should also try *Buchteln* or *Wuchteln*, yeast buns often filled with plum jam, and from Hungary the *Palatschinken*, pancakes filled

Viennese Sausage Stands

They all go for it: society ladies in posh frocks, night owls, opera buffs, work-ers – they all stand together at the Sausage Stand. Typical fare includes frankfurters (usual hot dog sausage), *Debreziner* (thin and spicy), *Bratwurst* (hunky thick fried sausage) and *Kasekrainer* (thick and made with meat and cheese). *Burenwurst* is a sort of boiled *Bratwurst*. There are stands all over town, including: **Albertina Wurstelstand**, Augustinerplatz, 8am–4am; **Hoher Markt** (the most famous), Marc Aurel Strasse, 7am–4am; **Zur Oper**, Kärntnerstrasse 10am–5am.

A nice helping of *Apfelstrudel* at Café Central

with jam or nuts. And don't forget the *Apfelstrudel*, a flaky pastry filled with thinly sliced apples, raisins and cinnamon.

Finally, there's one of the most famous and sinfully delicious chocolate cakes in the world, the *Sachertorte*. Join in the endless debate over whether or not it should be split into two layers and where the apricot jam should go.

Wines and Wine Gardens

Wine in Vienna is almost always white, which the Viennese drink with meat and fish alike. The best known of Austrian white wines, the *Gumpoldskirchner*, has the full body and bouquet of its southern vineyards. The Viennese give equal favour to their own *Grinzinger, Nussdorfer, Sieveringer* and *Neustifter*. From the Danube Valley, with an extra natural sparkle, come the *Kremser, Dürnsteiner* and *Langenloiser*.

Of the reds, the *Vöslauer*, produced in Bad Vöslau near Baden, and the *Kalterersee*, imported from South Tyrol (now

Alto Adige in Italy), are about the best. *Blaufränkisch* and *Zweigelt* are also reliable standbys. To enjoy these wines in their original state, they should be ordered *herb* (dry). Often the producers will sweeten them for the foreign palate unless you specify otherwise. Perhaps the most pleasant thing about Viennese wine is the way in which it is drunk.

The Viennese have created a splendid institution, the *Heuriger*, where you can sip white wine on mild evenings under the stars. Winemakers are allowed by law to sell a certain amount of their new wine (also called *Heuriger*) directly to the public. They announce the new wine by hanging out a sprig of pine over the door and a sign saying *Ausg'steckt* (open). The *Heuriger* of **Grinzing** are extremely popular, but many of the best ones are out in **Nussdorf, Ober-Sievering** and **Neustift**. *Heuriger* gardens are generally open from midafternoon until late in the evening and at weekends for lunch. The season runs from March to October.

The local *Gösser* beer presents a fair challenge to the powerful *Pilsner Urquell* imported from the Czech Republic. Among the brandies you should try the Hungarian *Barack* (apricot) and Serbian *Slivovitz* (plum).

Chocolate-rich *Sachertorte*

Coffee and the Kaffeehaus

The varieties of coffee in Vienna are virtually endless, and there are names for every shade from black to white. Ask for *einen kleinen Mokka* and you'll get a small, strong black coffee and stamp yourself as someone of French or Italian taste. A *Kapuziner*, topped

Waitress service at Café Demel

with generous dollops of cream, is more Viennese; *ein Brauner*, with just a dash of milk, is as Viennese as can be. *Eine Melange* (pronounced 'melanksch'), a mixture of milk and coffee, is designed for sensitive stomachs; *ein Einspänner*, with whipped cream in a tall glass, is for aunts on Sundays; *ein Türkischer*, prepared semi-sweet in a copper pot, is for addicts of the Balkan Connection.

The Viennese *Kaffeehaus* dates back to the 17th century when, depending on which legend you choose, either a Polish spy named Kulczycki or a Greek merchant named Theodat opened the first café with a stock of coffee beans captured from the Turks. By the time of Maria Theresa the town was full of coffee houses, fashionable and shady, where gentry and intellectuals mingled. Some developed their own particular clientele – writers, artists, politicians – while the most prominent (Griensteidl, Café Central, Herrenhof) attracted all types.

Impeccable service

After a post-war lull, the institution made a grand comeback. In the Innere Stadt, the renovated **Café Central** and the more sedate **Griensteidl** are thriving once again. With chandeliers adorning the ceiling, the former imperial bakery **Café Demel** on the Kohlmarkt is said to have the best cakes in town. **Café Hawelka**, at Dorotheergasse 6, once popular with artists and antiques dealers, has become a hangout for the younger crowd. Artists now prefer **Alt-Wien**, at Bäckerstrasse 9, and the **Kleines Café**, Franziskanerplatz 3, with its superb interior design by architect Hermann Czech. Intellectuals have followed the example of the late Thomas Bernhard in favouring **Café Bräunerhof**, at Stallburg-gasse 2. This café is also popular with music-lovers for its weekend chamber-music recitals. In the 6th District, **Café Sperl**, Gumpendorfer Strasse 11, is an elegant 100-year-old establishment with marble tables, *Jugendstil* chairs and an endless row of newspapers (including *The Times*, *Le Monde* and *La Stampa*).

To Help You Order...

Waiter, waitress, please!	**Bedienung, bitte!**
Could we have a table?	**Wir hätten gerne einen Tisch.**
May I see the menu, please?	**Die Speisekarte, bitte.**

The bill please.   **Zahlen bitte.**
I would like...   **Ich möchte gerne...**

Beer	**ein Bier**	Menu	**Speisekarte**
Bread	**Brot**	Milk	**Milch**
Butter	**Butter**	Mineral	
Cheese	**Käse**	water	**Mineralwasser**
Dessert	**Nachtisch**	Potatoes	**Erdäpfel**
Fish	**Fisch**	Salad	**Salat**
Fruit	**Obst**	Soup	**Suppe**
Fruit juice	**Fruchtsaft**	Sugar	**Zucker**
Ice cream	**Eis**	Tea	**Tee**
Meat	**Fleisch**	Wine	**Wein**

...and Read the Menu

Auflauf	casserole	**Kuchen**	cake
Backhendl	sautéed chicken	**Lamm**	lamb
Debreziner	spicy sausage	**Leber**	liver
Ente	duck	**Marillen-**	apricot
Erdbeeren	strawberries	**knödel**	dumpling
Faschiertes	minced meat	**Nockerln**	small
Frittaten-	broth with		dumplings
suppe	sliced crêpes	**Paradieser**	tomatoes
Gans	goose	**Rahm**	cream
Guglhupf	coffee cake	**Rindfleisch**	beef
Gurke	gherkin	**Rostbraten**	pot roast
Kaiser-	cured pork	**Rotkraut**	red cabbage
fleisch	spare ribs	**Schinken**	ham
Kaiser-	pancake with	**Schweine-**	pork
schmarrn	fruit compote	**fleisch**	
Kalb	veal	**Topfen**	cream cheese
Kirschen	cherries	**Zwetschken**	plums
Knödeln	dumplings	**Zwiebeln**	onions

HANDY TRAVEL TIPS

An A–Z Summary of Practical Information

A

ACCOMMODATION (For Recommended Hotels, see page 126)

The Vienna Tourist Board publishes a list of hotels, *Pensionen* (guest houses) and *Saison-Hotels* (student hostels used as hotels from July to September) with details about amenities, prices and classifications. You can pick it up, along with an excellent free city map, from the Austrian Tourist Board in your country or from travel agents. Tourist information offices in Vienna *(see page 123)* can book rooms for you, for a small fee. Telephone assistance is available year-round through Wien-Hotels, tel: 24 555; fax: 24 555 666; or log on to the Tourist Board's website, www.info.wien. If you do cancel your reservation, the hotel has a right to charge a cancellation fee.

The friendly atmosphere of a pension in Vienna makes it popular for longer stays, though, as with some of the cheaper hotels, not all of them have rooms with private baths. Apartments are also available for longer stays. It is always advisable to book ahead, especially for travel from Easter to the end of September, and at Christmas and New Year. It is also possible to stay in private homes on a bed-and-breakfast basis. This is an especially attractive option in some of the smaller villages around Vienna. The famous old luxury hotels around the Opera are often fully booked by a long-established clientele, so reservations are necessary well in advance. However 'old-fashioned' they may appear on the outside, Vienna's luxury hotels often have full, state-of-the-art business, sports and fitness facilities.

a guest house	**eine Pension**
a single/double room	**ein Einzel-/Doppelzimmer**
with/without bath (shower)	**mit/ohne Bad (Dusche)**
What's the rate per night?	**Was kostet eine Übernachtung?**

AIRPORT *(Flughafen)*

Wien-Schwechat Airport, www.viennaairport.com, about 20km (12 miles) from the centre of Vienna, handles domestic and international flights.

The City Airport Train (CAT), which leaves every 30 minutes, provides a high-speed (16 minutes) connection to the City Air Terminal at Landstrasse (Wien Mitte). There is also the Schnell-bahn (S-Bahn), which takes longer but is much cheaper. Airport shuttle buses leave every 30 minutes for Schwedenplatz or UNO-City. The Airport Service Wien is a private shuttle service that takes you to your exact address (tel: 676 351 6420, www.airport service.at).

Where can I find a taxi?	**Wo finde ich ein Taxi?**
How much is it to the centre?	**Wieviel kostet es ins Zentrum?**
Does this bus go to the railway station?	**Fährt dieser Bus zum Bahnhof?**

B

BICYCLE RENTAL *(Fahrrad-Verleih)*

With the increase in bicycle lanes, cycling is growing in popularity among tourists as well as local citizens as a way of beating the traffic snarls.

The Ringstrasse makes a perfect circular route for seeing the sights, and the Wienerwald on the city outskirts has 230km (144 miles) of cycle paths through the woods – for leisurely family excursions or mountain-bikers. Bicycles are available to rent from bike hire shops and at main-line railway stations. Pedal Power (www.pedalpower.at) hires out bikes and organises guided tours (advance booking required).

BUDGETING FOR YOUR TRIP

To give you an idea of what to expect, here is a list of average prices in euros (€). They can only be approximate, however, as in Austria, too, inflation creeps relentlessly up. One way to save money is the Vienna Card *(see opposite)*, available from the Tourist Information Office *(see page 124)*. It provides discounts on transport, sightseeing, shopping and entertainment.

Airport. City Airport Train (CAT) to city centre €8 single, €15 return; S-Bahn €4.50.

Bicycle rental. Adult €27, child €19, student €21 for one day.

Car rental. (advance booking from abroad) from €70 per day, from €250 for three days.

Entertainment. Cinema from €8, nightclub from about €40, disco from about €5.

Guides. From €100 for half a day.

Hotels. (double room with bath or shower per night, including breakfast). ***** €200–750, **** €150–250, *** €100–200, ** €80–150, * €50–100 *(see Recommended Hotels, page 126)*.

Meals. The average cost of a standard meal, including a glass of wine is between €18 and €25 per person.

Museums. Entrance fees vary considerably. Concessions are available at many museums for holders of the Vienna Card *(see page 104)*. Entrance for children under six is free. There is a reduction for schoolchildren (passport required) and students (international student identity card required).

Public transport. €1.70 for single ticket, €5.70 for a 24-hour ticket, €13.60 for a 72-hour ticket. Children under six years old travel free. Children under 15 are allowed to travel free on Sundays and public holidays and during the Viennese school holidays on presentation of an identity card.

Sightseeing. *Fiaker:* about €30 for a short tour and €60 for a longer one (although not all that much longer); *MS Vindobona* motorboat: from about €13.

Taxis. Meter starts at around €2, €1 per km or €0.20 per minute.
Tickets. Concerts €5–€55; opera €5–€185; Spanish Riding School morning training, adults €12, senior citizens €9, children €6; performances, €23–€116, www.spanische-reitschule.com; Vienna Boys' Choir €5–€20, hmk@aon.at.
Vienna Card. The Vienna Card provides reduced admission and other benefits at 180 museums and sights, theatres, concert halls, shops, restaurants, cafés and wine gardens *(Heuriger)*; unlimited travel by underground, bus and tram, and a reduction on the shuttle bus to/from the city centre.

The card costs €18.50 and is valid for 72 hours. It can be purchased at Vienna Airport and at hotels and tourist information offices, and by credit card, tel: 798 44 00-148.

C

CAMPING

For information about campsites, camping and caravanning, www.campsite.at is helpful if you can read German. Of camping sites located around the city, one is open all year: Wien West I/II, Hüttelbergstrasse 40 and 80, tel: 941 449 or 942 314. Other sites: Aktiv Camping Neue Donau, Am Kleehäufel, tel: 202 4010 (mid-May–Sept); Wien Süd, An der Au 2, tel: 888 4154 (July–Aug).

CAR RENTAL/HIRE (Autovermietung, see also DRIVING)

For travelling inside the city, parking would make a car more of a hindrance than an asset, but having a car is certainly useful for excursions out to the Wienerwald and the Danube Valley.

Though some local firms may offer lower prices than Avis, Budget, Europcar and Hertz, these international agencies are more likely to let you return the car elsewhere in the country at no extra cost. The best deal can usually be obtained through your travel agency or sometimes via your airline before leaving home.

Third-party insurance is compulsory, but full cover is recommended. To avoid unpleasant surprises, make sure the price quoted includes all the necessary insurance and taxes. To hire a car, you must show your driving licence (held for at least a year) and passport. You also need a major credit card, or a large deposit will be required. The minimum age for renting cars ranges from 20 to 23.

Avis, tel: 7007 32700, 32961, www.avis.at
Budget, tel: 7007 32711, 33659, www.budget.co.uk
Denzeldrive, tel: 0800 0800 800 (toll free), www.denzeldrive.at
Europcar, tel: 7007 333 16, www.europcar.at
Hertz, tel: 7007 32661, 32432, www.hertz.at

I'd like to rent a car	**Ich möchte bitte ein Auto mieten**
today	**für heute**
tomorrow	**für morgen**
for a week	**für eine Woche**

CLIMATE

Spring is Vienna's most pleasant season. Chestnut trees and white lilacs are in blossom for the city's music festival. In July and August the Viennese leave the city relatively free for visitors, and in autumn, the Wienerwald is in splendid colour for the *Heuriger* wine gardens, and the opera and theatre season in the city centre. Even in winter Vienna is worth the trip for a marvellous white Christmas, despite the cold east wind.

The chart shows Vienna's average monthly temperatures:

	J	F	M	A	M	J	J	A	S	O	N	D
°F	30	34	41	50	59	64	68	66	61	50	41	34
°C	-1	1	5	10	15	18	20	19	16	10	5	1

CLOTHING *(Kleidung)*

For the extremes of Vienna's weather, take light cottons for the very hot summer afternoons and your warmest woollens for the bitter winter. That wind off the steppes can whip through at any time; so even in summer, for an occasional cool evening, take a sweater and raincoat. The Viennese like to dress up for the theatre, concerts and opera, but a dark suit or cocktail dress is nearly always appropriate. A dinner jacket or evening dress may be worn on special occasions, such as for premieres and galas.

CRIME AND SAFETY (See also EMERGENCIES and POLICE)

Austria's crime and theft rate is quite low compared to other parts of Europe. Don't leave valuable objects on display in your car and take the same precautions as you would at home. If your passport is stolen, the police will give you a certificate to take to your consulate.

I want to report a theft.	**Ich möchte einen Diebstahl melden.**

CUSTOMS *(Zoll)* AND ENTRY REQUIREMENTS

A valid passport is required for entry. Visitors from European Union (EU) countries, the US, Canada, Australia and New Zealand do not require a visa. See www.austria.org.uk for further information from the Austrian Embassy in London.

Currency restrictions. There are no restrictions on the import and export of national and foreign currencies.

VAT reimbursement. For purchases over a specified amount, non-EU citizens are entitled to reclaim the value-added tax *(Mehrwert-steuer)* if you are taking the goods out of the EU. The salesperson must complete form 'U 34', which you will need to present on departure to airport or border customs officials for stamping. Then you can post the form to the shop for reimbursement by cheque or bank-order.

| I've nothing to declare. | **Ich habe nichts zu verzollen.** |
| It's for my personal use. | **Das ist für meinen persönlichen Gebrauch.** |

D

DRIVING (See also CAR RENTAL/HIRE)

To bring your car into Austria you will need:

   valid driving licence (national licence for Europeans);

   car registration papers;

   national identity sticker for your car;

   red warning triangle in case of breakdown;

   first-aid kit.

Road conditions are by and large very good in Austria, only remote country roads are not paved.

Driving regulations. Drive on the right, pass on the left. Although drivers in Austria follow the same basic rules which apply in other countries that drive on the right, there are some rules that might differ somewhat:

• you must wear seat-belts;

• children under the age of 12 may not sit in front, and must use a special safety seat;

• on the motorway *(Autobahn)* passing another vehicle on its right is prohibited;

• vehicles coming from the right have priority at crossroads without other signals;

• trams have priority, even when coming from the left;

• vehicles must halt behind trams when they are slowing down to stop and when loading or unloading passengers;

- it is prohibited to use your horn (day or night) in town;
- motorcyclists must wear crash helmets and use dipped headlights throughout the day;
- drunken driving is a very serious offence in Austria. The permissible alcohol level in the blood is 0.8 percent.

Speed limits. On motorways (expressways) 130km/h (81mph) or 100km/h (62mph); on other roads 100km/h or 80km/h (50mph); in built-up areas 50km/h (31mph); with caravan (trailer) 80km/h (50mph) on the open road; with studded tires 100km/h (62mph) on motorways, 80km/h (50mph) on other roads.

Parking. In streets with tram tracks, parking is prohibited from 8pm to 5am from mid-December to the end of March for snow clearance. If at all possible, use public transport within the Gürtel (outer ring road) since one-way streets and traffic jams add confusion within the city, where there is a lack of parking space. To park in 'blue' zones you will need parking tickets, valid from 8am to 6pm for up to 90 minutes. Tickets are available in banks and tobacco shops *(Tabaktrafik)*.

Breakdowns. Austrian automobile clubs offer 24-hour breakdown service to all drivers on motorways and main roads; ÖAMTC, tel:

driving licence	**Führerschein**
car registration papers	**Zulassungsschein**
green card	**Grüne Karte**
Where's the nearest car park, please?	**Wo ist der nächste Parkplatz, bitte?**
Can I park here?	**Darf ich hier parken?**
Are we on the right road for...?	**Sind wir auf der richtigen Strasse nach...?**
Check the oil/tires/battery, please.	**Öl/Reifen/Batterie prüfen, bitte.**
I've had a breakdown.	**Ich habe eine Panne.**
There's been an accident.	**Es ist ein Unfall passiert.**

120, www.oeamtc.at; ARBÖ, tel: 123, www.arboe.at.

Fuel and oil. There are plenty of petrol stations, some of them self-service. In Vienna, most service stations close at night, but you can fill up very late at the main entrances to the city.

Road signs. Most road signs employed in Austria are international, but here are some written signs you might come across:

Anfang	(Parking) Start	**Licht einschalten**	Use headlights
Ausfahrt	Exit		
Aussicht	Viewpoint	**Ortsende**	Town ends
Bau- arbeiten	Road works	**Parken erlaubt**	Parking allowed
		Rechts, links einbiegen	Turn right, left
Einbahn- strasse	One way	**Rollsplitt**	Loose gravel
Ende	(Parking) End	**Sackgasse**	No through road
Fahrbahn- wechsel	Change lanes	**Spital**	Hospital
		Steinschlag	Falling stones
Fussgänger	Pedestrians	**Umleitung**	Diversion
Gefahr	Danger	**Vorfahrt**	Priority
Geradeaus	Straight on	**Vorsicht**	Caution
Glatteis	Slippery roads	**Werktags von 7 bis 17 Uhr**	Weekdays 7am to 5pm
Halten- verboten-	No stopping	**Zufahrt gestattet**	Entrance permitted

E

ELECTRICITY

You'll need an adapter for most British and US plugs: Austrian sockets have round holes. Electricity supplies are 220 volt, and US equipment will require a transformer. Shaver outlets are generally dual voltage.

EMBASSIES AND CONSULATES

Contact your consulate or embassy only for real emergencies, such as loss of a passport or all your money, a serious accident or trouble with the police.

Australia Mattiellistrasse 2, A-1040 Vienna, tel: 50674.
Canada Laurenzerberg 2, 1010 Vienna, tel: 531 383000,
Ireland Rotenturmstrasse 16–18, 1010 Vienna, tel: 715 4246.
New Zealand Springsiedelgasse 28, 1090 Vienna, tel: 318 8505.
UK Jauresgasse 12, 1030 Vienna, tel: 71613-0.
US (Embassy) Boltzmanngasse 16, 1090 Vienna, tel: 31339-0; (Consulate) Gartenbaupromenade 2, 1010 Vienna, tel: 512 5835.

| Where is the British Embassy? | **Wo ist die britische Botschaft?** |

EMERGENCIES (See also CRIME AND SAFETY and POLICE)

The most important Viennese emergency service numbers are given below.

Police emergency **133**
Fire **122**
Ambulance, first aid **144**
Pharmacist on duty **1550**
Emergency medical service **141**
Emergency dentist **512 2078**

I need a doctor/dentist.	**Ich brauche einen Arzt/ Zahnarzt.**
ambulance	**Krankenwagen**
Fire!	**Feuer!**
Help!	**Hilfe!**
hospital	**Spital**
police	**Polizei**

G

GAY AND LESBIAN TRAVELLERS

This sophisticated capital has a relatively friendly attitude towards gays and lesbians. Since 1996, the Regenbogen (Gay Rainbow) Parade has been held every June on the Ringstrasse. A list of restaurants, hotels and bars which welcome gays and lesbians is provided in the *Gay City Map,* available at some bars and hotels or directly from the publisher: BG Verlag, Mariahilferstrasse 123/3, 1060 Vienna. Two places for information are: Hosi Zentrum, Novaragasse 40. 1040 Wien, tel: 216 6604, www.hosiwien.at, and Rosa Lila Villa, 6, Linke Wienzeile 102, tel: 586 8150, www.villa.at.

GETTING THERE

By Air

Scheduled flights. There is regular service to Vienna from various centres in the UK. Austrian Airlines (www.aua.com) operates scheduled flights from Heathrow; British Airways (www.ba.com) has flights from Heathrow. Lauda-Air (www.laudaair.com) has occasional flights from Edinburgh and Glasgow. Flying time from London is two and a half hours. The low-cost airline Easyjet (www.easyjet.com) flies from Gatwick to Vienna, while both Easyjet and Ryanair (www.ryanair.com) operate a service to Salzburg. The train journey from Salzburg to Vienna takes three hours. Various firms offer Vienna as a city break.

In addition to non-stop flights from New York and Chicago, there is a scheduled service from more than 40 American cities as well as a dozen cities in Canada to European gateway destinations from which you can make connections to Vienna.

Charter flights. Cheap charter flights are available from the UK. Accommodation is not generally included.

Charters operate from a selection of North American cities, including ABC (Advanced Booking Charter) flights and OTC (One-

Stop Inclusive Tour Charter) package deals, which include return flights, hotel accommodation, selected meals and sightseeing. In addition, a number of British and American tour operators have individual and group packages to Austria offering stays of from two days to two weeks in Vienna. Consult your travel agent for details.

By Car

The quickest route to Vienna from the UK is via Calais through Brussels, Cologne, Nuremburg, Passau and Linz, although there are more attractive routes, such as *die romantische Strasse* (the Romantic Road), via Rothenburg ob der Tauber, through the countryside. There are regular daily car ferry departures from Dover to Calais, or you can put your car on the train and travel through the Channel Tunnel from Folkestone to Calais in 35 minutes.

Depending from which direction you come, you might be able to put your car on the train for part of the journey. In the summer a car-train *(Autozug)* service links Vienna with cities in Germany and Italy. Arriving with the car-train allows you to avoid traffic jams around Vienna and brings you close to the town centre.

The Austrian Federal Railways (www.oebb.at) operates car-trains between Vienna and Bischofshofen, Feldkirch (overnight service with couchettes also available), Linz, Villach and Innsbruck and Salzburg (both during the skiing season only).

By Rail

The Köln–Vienna sleeper is the easiest way to reach Austria from London (connect via Brussels on Eurostar) and it takes about 13 hours; the entire trip, London to Vienna, takes about 20 hours. The cabins are very comfortable and couchettes are also available. Book on-line at (www.bahn.de/citynightline).

The Austrian National Railpass *(Bundes-Netzkarte)* allows unlimited travel on Austrian Railways for one month. Contact Austrian Federal Railways for details (www.oebb.at).

By Coach

For details of coach services to Vienna from London and other European cities contact Eurolines (www.eurolines.co.uk).

GUIDES AND TOURS *(Fremdenführer; Rundfahrten)*

The most romantic tour of Vienna is in the famous horse-drawn *Fiaker* cab. These are usually parked at the Heldenplatz, Stephansplatz, or near the Albertina and will take you around the major sightseeing spots – the younger drivers may provide a running commentary in English as you ride. Make sure you agree on the cost of the trip before you begin. The price of a tram ticket will take you right round the Ringstrasse, but without commentary.

Vienna-Line bus tours, with an English-speaking hostess, are conveniently run on a hop-on/hop-off basis at 13 stops along the sightseeing route, starting from the Staatsoper. An uninterrupted tour lasts 2½ hours, but you can spread it over two days. Tickets can be purchased in many hotels or from Vienna Sightseeing Tours, 3, Stelzhammergasse 4/11, tel: 712 46 83 0.

The Tourist Information Board organises guided **theme tours on foot** (*Wiener Spaziergänge* (www.wienguide.at), often with English-speaking guides. Each tour lasts approximately 90 minutes. They cover all manner of special interests: Medieval Vienna, Hundertwasser and modern architecture, Jewish Vienna, *Jugendstil*, Amusing Vienna with tales and anecdotes. One particularly interesting walk is the *Musikmeile* (Music Mile). This is a classical music walk from Theater an der Wien to Stephansplatz, following stars embedded in the pavement that commemorate great personalities of classical music. You can also enjoy *Verliebt in Wien* (Vienna with love) and *Der Dritte Mann* (The Third Man), which follows in the footsteps of the film (which is shown quite often at the Burgkino, www. burgkino.at). There are guided tours of the sewers as well, but if all this is too sober, why not try *Ein luderleben der liebesdienerinnen* (The Erotic Vienna:

a dissolute life of the tart)? Or alternatively, the Josefine Mutzen-bacher Walk, which is humorous and deemed unsuitable for children, despite the bestseller about Josefine's life having been written by Felix Salten, the author renowned for writing *Bambi* (see www.wienfuehrung.com).

There are also tram and boat tours.

Most hotels can arrange – at a price – for English-speaking guides or interpreters to accompany you on your way around the city. Otherwise contact the Vienna Tourist Board for more information or the service below:

Vienna Guide Service, tel: 786 2400, www.viennaguideservice.at.

We'd like an English-speaking guide.	**Wir möchten einen englisch-sprachigen Fremdenführer.**
I need an English interpreter.	**Ich brauche einen Dolmetscher für Englisch.**
How long will the ride take?	**Wie lange dauert die Fahrt?**
What does it cost?	**Was kostet es?**

H

HEALTH AND MEDICAL CARE *(Ärztliche Hilfe)*

You should have few worries in Vienna. The tap water is perfectly safe to drink. Ask your insurance company before leaving home if medical treatment in Austria is covered by your policy. Pack whatever prescription drugs you may need, as you may not find exactly the same in Vienna. If you are a resident of an EU country you should obtain a European Health Insurance Card before travelling or you will be liable to pay the full cost of medical treatment.

Most pharmacies *(Apotheke)* are open Monday to Friday and Saturday morning *(see* OPENING HOURS*).* For night and Sunday service, pharmacies display the address of the nearest shop re-

maining on duty. To find out which are open, tel: **1550** (see also
EMERGENCIES).

Where is there a pharmacy on duty?	**Wo ist die diensthabende Apotheke?**

L

LANGUAGE

Austria is German-speaking, but English is also very widely understood and spoken. If you don't speak German, don't forget to ask *'Sprechen Sie Englisch?'* (Do you speak English?) before plunging ahead. A gentle effort at *'Entschuldigen Sie bitte'* (Excuse me, please) gets you a long way. The *Berlitz German Phrase Book and Dictionary* covers most situations you're likely to encounter in Austria.

LOST PROPERTY (Fundamt)

The city lost property office is at Wasagasse 22, tel: 313 44 92 11; open Mon–Fri, 8am–noon.

I've lost my passport/wallet/handbag	**Ich habe meinen Pass/meine Brieftasche/Handtasche verloren.**

M

MAPS

The Tourist Information Board gives away excellent street-maps of the city. Most useful will always be a large-scale map of the *Innere Stadt* (Inner City) and of the U-Bahn network. The one other place for which you will need a map is the Kunsthistorisches (Fine Arts) Museum – they can be obtained for free at the information desk.

MEDIA

Major hotels and most kiosks in the First District sell English-language daily newspapers from London, *International Herald Tribune*, *Wall Street Journal* and *USA Today*, and the news magazines.

TV in the major hotels usually has CNN and BBC World news services, along with other major European channels. The state-run broadcaster for TV and radio is ÖRF (www.orf.at).

Vienna Tourist Board's *Monatsprogramm* provides full monthly cultural listings. German-speakers get a less formal, fresher view of the city's events, along with a full restaurant guide, with the first-rate weekly *Falter* magazine (similar to London's *Time Out* or New York's *Village Voice*).

MONEY *(Geld)*

Austria's monetary unit is the euro, symbolised €. The euro is divided into 100 cents. Banknotes in denominations of 5, 10, 20, 50, 100, 200 and 500 euros are in circulation. There are coins to the value of 1 and 2 euros and 1, 2, 5, 10, 20 and 50 cents.

Banks and currency exchange. Foreign currency can be changed in practically all banks and savings banks *(Sparkasse)*. You can also change money at travel agencies and hotels, but the rate will not be as good. The quickest way to obtain cash is to use one of the many ATMs *(Geldautomat)*. Major credit cards are accepted in most hotels, restaurants and shops in the tourist districts.

Bureaux de change are usually open from early morning (some from 6.30am) until late afternoon or evening. Some are open at the weekend, including those at the airport, Südbahnhof, Westbahnhof, City Air Terminal, Stephansplatz and Opernpassage.

Travellers' cheques *(Reisescheck)* are welcome almost everywhere, but, again, the rates are best in banks.

I want to change some pounds/dollars	**Ich möchte Pfund/ Dollar wechseln.**
Do you accept travellers' cheques?	**Nehmen Sie Reiseschecks an?**
Do you have any change, please?	**Haben Sie Kleingeld, bitte?**
Where's the nearest ATM, please?	**Wo ist der nächste Geldautomat, bitte?**

OPENING HOURS

Shops. Most small places are open from 9am (grocery stores an hour earlier) to 6pm with a break for lunch. Major department stores do business from 8am–6pm, and in some cases 8pm, but supermarkets close for about two hours at lunch. Most shops close on Saturday afternoon, though some remain open until 5pm. Most shops remain closed on Sunday. Shops in railway stations are open daily 7am–10.30pm.

Museums. Hours vary considerably (see individual listings in the Where to Go section).

Banks. Mon–Fri 8am–3pm (Thur to 5.30pm). Most branches close 12.30–1.30pm.

Post offices. Mon–Fri 8am–6pm. For 24-hour service, see POST OFFICE.

Pharmacies. Mon–Fri 8am–noon, 2–6pm; Sat 8am–noon.

P

POLICE (*Polizei*, see also CRIME AND SAFETY and EMERGENCIES)

Vienna's police wear green caps and jackets with black trousers, and drive white cars. Traffic police wear white caps and, in summer, white jackets. Street parking is supervised by *Politessen* (traffic wardens) in blue jackets and white hats. Police on motorcycles are popularly known as 'white mice' *(weisse Mäuse)*.

If you are fined for any reason, the police have the right to ask you to pay on the spot.

In emergencies, call **133**.

Where is the nearest police station, please?	**Wo ist die nächste Polizeiwache, bitte?**

POST OFFICE *(Postamt)*

Apart from regular post office hours, post offices at main railway stations (Westbahnhof, Südbahnhof and Franz Josefs-Bahnhof) are open day and night. Other offices offering this 24-hour service for registered, air and express mail (with a small extra charge): Central Post Office, Fleischmarkt 19, and Central Telegraph Office, Börseplatz 1. Stamps are also available at tobacco shops *(Tabaktrafik)*.

express (special delivery)	**Express/Eilbote**
airmail	**Luftpost**
Have you any mail for...?	**Haben Sie Post für...?**
A stamp for this letter/ postcard, please.	**Eine Marke für diesen Brief/ diese Postkarte, bitte.**
I want to fax a letter to...	**Ich möchte einen Brief nach... faxen.**

PUBLIC HOLIDAYS *(Feiertage)*

Austria observes 14 public holidays a year on which banks, museums, official services and many restaurants are closed. On Good Friday, a holiday for Protestants only, shops remain open.

January 1	*Neujahrstag*	New Year's Day
January 6	*Heilige Drei Könige*	Twelfth Night
May 1	*Tag der Arbeit*	Labour Day
August 15	*Mariä Himmelfahrt*	Assumption
October 26	*Nationalfeiertag*	National Holiday
	(Tag der Fahne)	(Flag Day)
November 1	*Allerheiligen*	All Saints' Day
December 8	*Unbefleckte*	Immaculate
	Empfängnis	Conception
December 25	*Weihnachten*	Christmas Day
December 26	*Stefanstag*	St Stephen's Day
Movable dates:	*Karfreitag*	Good Friday
	Ostermontag	Easter Monday
	Christi Himmelfahrt	Ascension Day
	Pfingstmontag	Whit Monday
	Fronleichnam	Corpus Christi

On 24 December (Christmas Eve) theatres and cinemas are closed all day and shops, restaurants and coffee houses close at midday.

Are you open tomorrow?   **Haben Sie morgen geöffnet?**

PUBLIC TRANSPORT

Maps for buses, trams and U-Bahn (subway) are available at main stops as well as at the central public transport information offices at Karlsplatz and Stephansplatz.

Tickets can be bought from a conductor or a machine on trams and buses, from the booking office or a machine for mainline or city trains. A single ticket for a journey by tram, bus and under-ground, which covers changes made without interruption, costs €1.70. Tickets can be bought in advance from a tobacconist's *(Tabaktrafik)* or transport offices *(Verkehrsbetriebe)*. Travel passes are available for 24 hours (€5.70) and 72 hours (€13.60).

Also worth considering is the Vienna Card, a 72-hour ticket currently costing €18.50, which is valid on all public transport and entitles the holder to discounts at museums and other attractions (see BUDGETING FOR YOUR TRIP).

Trams *(Strassenbahn)*. With some 35 tram routes, this is Vienna's most important form of public transport. On most trams (and buses) the driver serves as the conductor. These vehicles carry a blue sign front and rear with the word *Schaffnerlos* (without conductor). If you have a ticket, enter by the door marked *Entwerter* and have it stamped; otherwise get in at the front and buy your ticket from the vending machine. For trams with conductors, enter at the rear to buy a ticket or have it stamped. The most useful lines are:

1 and 2 around the Ringstrasse.

38 from Schottentor to Grinzing.

52 and 58 from the Westbahnhof to the city centre.

Buses. The airport bus service runs between the City Air Terminal at Landstrasse Hauptstrasse (Hilton Hotel) and the airport every 20 or 30 minutes. Allow half-an-hour for the journey. The main city centre routes are:

1a from Schottentor to Stephansplatz.

2a from Burgring to Graben.

3a from Schottenring to Schwarzenbergplatz.

U-Bahn (underground). Five lines cover all the main parts of the city. Tickets can be purchased from machines or ticket offices. The lines are:

U1 Kagran–Stephansplatz–Karlsplatz–Reumannplatz.

U2 Schottenring–Volkstheater–Karlsplatz.

U3 Ottakring–Stephansplatz–Landstrasse–Simmering.

U4 Hütteldorf–Karlsplatz–Schwedenplatz–Heiligenstadt.

U6 Floridsdorf–Spittelau–Westbahnhof–Meidling–Philadelphia-brücke–Siebenherten.

Schnellbahn (S-Bahn). Rapid transit suburban trains depart from the Südbahnhof for outlying districts. The unit fare applies in the central zone, standard fares outside. Other points of departure are Wien Nord and Wien Mitte. The S-Bahn also connects to the airport, as does the City Airport Train (CAT; see AIRPORT).

R

RELIGION

Austria is predominantly Roman Catholic. Sunday Mass in some churches is accompanied by orchestral and choral works. Consult a newspaper under *Kirchenmusik* for exact times.

English-language Catholic Mass is held at 11am at Votivkirche, Rooseveltplatz 8, tel: 408 5050 14. There is an Anglican/Episcopal Church at Jauresgasse 17–19, tel: 720 7973. Jewish services take place at the Stadttempel, Seitenstettengasse 4, tel: 531 0415.

T

TAXIS

Book in advance through your hotel receptionist or by calling one of the following numbers: tel: 31 300/40 100/60 160/81 400. If you want to go beyond the city limits, negotiate the fare in advance.

TELEPHONES

Austria's country code is **43**, Vienna's area code is **(0)1**, dropping the 0 for calls from abroad. For **international calls** from Vienna, dial **00** before the country code (**44** for UK, **1** for US), then the area code and number of your destination.

Use call centres or telephone booths with pre-paid cards. Phone cards *(Telefonwertkarte)* are available from post offices and tobacconists; costs vary so shop around for the best buy. Telephone booths all have multilingual instructions. Calls are cheaper 6pm–8am and on Saturday, Sunday and public holidays. Hotels often charge double the public phone rate to make a call.

| Directory enquiries (local) | 11811 |
| Directory enquiries (long-distance) | 11814 |

TICKETS *(Karten)*

Music. Tickets for performances can be obtained at private ticket agencies *(Theaterkartenbüro)* throughout the city, as well as at major hotels, but these will cost at least 22 percent more. It is best (and cheapest) to book directly with the opera house, theatre or concert hall. The city authority website www.wien.gv.at/english/culture/ticketing.htm has links to the individual booking services of numerous cultural institutions and events, including music.

Tickets for some of the Wiener Philharmoniker orchestra are only available through subscription and the waiting lists are long. Tickets for other concerts performed by the orchestra can be booked in advance: Wiener Philharmoniker, Bösendorferstrasse 12, 1010 Vienna, www.wienerphilharmoniker.at.

For concerts at the Musikverein tickets and returns are often available on the day and just before the performance at the box office at Bösendorferstrasse 12 (www.musikverein.at).

Spanish Riding School. Ticket applications should be sent at least six months in advance to: Spanische Reitschule, Michaelerplatz 1, 1010 Vienna, www.spanische-reitschule.com. Tickets can be bought on the day for the morning training sessions.

Opera and Theatre. The best place for opera tickets is the National Theatre ticket office *(Österreichischer Bundestheaterverband, Bestellbüro,* www.bundestheater.at). It sells tickets seven days ahead for opera (Staatsoper), operetta (Volksoper), Burgtheater and Akademietheater performances (closed in July and August). You can reserve tickets at least three weeks before the performance by writing to: Bundestheaterkassen, Goethegasse 1, 1010 Vienna. For information the number to call is 514 440. It is also possible to book tickets on-line. Standing-room tickets are sold for evening performances, only at the box office of the individual theatres on the day prior to the performance.

Vienna Boys' Choir *(Wiener Sängerknaben).* Obtain tickets in advance at the Hofburg Kapelle on Friday 5–7pm for Sunday performances, or reserve at least two months in advance from: Hofmusikkapelle, Hofburg, Schweizerhof, 1010 Vienna; www.wsk.at. The choir can also be heard every Friday at the Konzerthaus in May, June, September and October.

TIME ZONES

Austria is on Central European Time (GMT+1). In summer, clocks move ahead one hour, and the time difference looks like this:

New York	London	**Vienna**	Jo'burg	Sydney	Auckland
6am	11am	**noon**	noon	8pm	10pm

TIPPING

Since a service charge is included in hotel and restaurant bills, tipping is not obligatory, but it is customary to add a tip of about 10 percent to the bill. It is also appropriate to give something extra to porters, cloakroom attendants and hotel maids for their services. Taxi drivers and hairdressers also expect a 10 percent tip.

TOILETS *(Toiletten)*

Public facilities can be found near important streets or squares, often in the pedestrian underpasses. Normally toilets in cafés can be used without ordering anything, but it is polite to ask. If hand towels and soap are used in public facilities, there is often a set fee rather than just tip. Have some small change ready in case the door is coin operated. Toilets may be labelled with *Damen* (Ladies) and *Herren* (Gentlemen).

TOURIST INFORMATION

The Austrian National Tourist Office/ANTO *(die Österreichische Fremdenverkehrswerbung)* has comprehensive information about what to see, when to go, and where to stay in and around Vienna; www.austria.info.

Australia: ANTO, 1st Floor, 36 Carrington Street, Sydney NSW 2000, tel: 9299 3621, fax: 9299 3808.

Canada: ANTO, 2 Bloor Street East, Suite 3330, Toronto, Ontario M4W 1A8, tel: (416) 967-3381, fax: (416) 967-4101.

Ireland: ANTO, Merrion Centre, Nutley Lane, Dublin 4, tel: 01 283 0488, fax: 01 283 0531.

UK: ANTO, 14 Cork Street, London W1X 1PF, tel: 020 7629 0461, fax: 020 7499 6038.

US: ANTO, PO Box 1142, New York, NY 10108-1142, tel: 212 944 6880, fax: 212 730 4568.

Vienna Tourist Board

The Tourist Information Office is located right behind the Vienna State Opera at Albertinaplatz 1/corner of Maysedergasse, tel: 24 555, fax: 24 555 666; open 9am–7pm daily. The office is able to book tickets, make hotel reservations, organise sightseeing trips and change money. You can also make room reservations and request free brochures over the phone. The Vienna Tourist Board's website www.info.wien.at offers a monthly preview and comprehensive database of events, online booking for hotels and pensions, and information for visitors with disabilities.

TRAVELLERS WITH DISABILITIES

Vienna has implemented a great many schemes to enable wheelchair access. Most hotels have wheelchair access and some have rooms adapted for disabled people, though it would be wise to question the manager before making a reservation, to ensure that the room is suitable. Older buses and trams are not accessible, though many U-Bahn stations are. The Vienna Tourist Board can provide up-to-date information. It has a list of sights and attractions with wheelchair access – the *Riesenrad* (Ferris wheel) is accessible. Local voluntary organisations may also offer help.

Fahrtendienst Haas, Karl Schäferstrasse 6, A-1210, tel: 27700, fax: 27700/30, www.members.aon.at/haas-bus, provides transport for wheelchair users.

WEBSITES

The Vienna Tourist Board has an excellent website at **www.wien. info** with pages in seven languages, including English, that give comprehensive information about forthcoming cultural, sporting and social events. The board also has an email address to which you can send English-language queries: inquiries@info.wien.at. For hotel reservations, e-mail wienhotels@info.wien.at.

www.austria.info The Austrian Tourist Board site.

www.wien.gv.at The City of Vienna's website, lists information on all aspects of life in the city and is available in English.

www.wienmuseum.at For city museums.

www.falter.at the website of *Falter* magazine, for listings (this site is in German only).

YOUTH HOSTELS *(Jugendherberge)*

There is a large, modern hostel near the Museums Quartier, with two and four beds to a room. You can obtain information about the other 100 hostels in Austria there. Or contact:

Austrian Youth Hostels Association, Helferstorferstrasse 4, A–1010 Vienna, tel: 533 1833, fax: 533 1833 85, www.jungehotels.at

Jugendherberge Myrthengasse, Myrthengasse 7, A-1070 Wien, tel: 523 6316

A popular backpacker's place is Wombats, Grangasse 6, A-1150. tel 897 2336, fax: 897 2577, www.wombats.at, near Mariahilferstrasse. It's bright and cheap with free linen.

Recommended Hotels

Vienna's hotels compare in quality to those of other major European capitals. However, shortage of accommodation, particularly during peak season – Christmas and New Year, and from Easter to the end of September – does mean that advance booking is advisable. Reservations may be made by telephone (country code 43 followed by area code 1), fax, letter, or the Internet, and are binding even if not confirmed in writing. Vienna's hotels used to be heavy on the chintz, frills and Biedermeier look, and while this is still prominent in recent years a number of classy design hotels have opened, giving a more contemporary face to the city.

The hotels listed here are placed in four categories based on the approximate price in euros per night for a double room with private bath or shower unless otherwise stated. A service charge and taxes are included in the price. Breakfast is generally included in the price, although check when you reserve as it is not always the case in the more expensive places, usually a buffet of various cold meats and cheeses, cereals, bread, rolls, jam and coffee. Always confirm prices when booking. All the hotels listed take major credit cards; wheelchair access where specified.

The district number precedes the street address.

€€€€	over 300 euros
€€€	200–300 euros
€€	120–200 euros
€	under 120 euros

THE INNERE STADT (DISTRICT 1)

Arenberg €€ 1, *Stubenring 2, tel: 01-512 5291, fax: 01-513 9356, www.arenberg.at*. The doyen among pensions (part of the Best Western group), set in an atmospheric Ringstrasse building with a plush, elegant atmosphere and excellent location. Popular with visiting actors and singers, whose photographs adorn the reception area, all rooms have satellite TV and direct-dial telephones, and breakfast is included in the price.

Astoria €€€ *1, Kärntnerstrasse 32–34, tel: 01-515 770, fax: 01-515 7782, www.austria-trend.at.* A civilised old hotel immediately behind the Staatsoper. The bedrooms are large and comfortable with traditional décor. Some of them are accessible to physically disabled guests.

Hotel Austria €€ *1, Am Fleischmarkt 20, tel: 01-515 23, fax: 01-5152 3506, www.hotelaustria-wien.at.* Newly reconditioned rooms in a very centrally placed hotel; those without bath are cheaper. An elegant, friendly and quiet hotel.

Bristol €€€€ *1, Kärntner Ring 1, tel: 01-515 160, fax: 01-5151 6550, www.starwoodhotels.com.* An art nouveau building dating from 1884 that is rather more intimate than many other five-star hotels. Its restaurant, the Korso, is known for its light Viennese cuisine and distinguished wine list. There are non-smoking rooms and wheelchair facilities for guests.

Do & Co €€€€ *1, Stephansplatz 12, tel: 01-24188, fax: 01-2418 8444, www.doco.com.* This über-chic design hotel occupies possibly the most prime site in Vienna, on the upper storeys of the Haas Haus opposite Stephansdom. Great service and amazing views from the Bang & Olufsen-equipped cool, minimalist rooms are complimented by one of the most popular bars (the Onyx) and restaurants in the city. Although the rack rates are pretty high there are usually good offers in low season.

Hollman Beletage €€ *1, Köllnerhofgasse 6, tel: 01-961 1961, fax: 01-9611 96033, www.hollmann-beletage.at.* It is hard to recommend this small (only seven large rooms) hotel enough. It is very central, and the rooms are modern, chic and beautifully kept. It has a laid back feel, the reception shuts down at night, leaving the guests to help themselves at the bar. It is excellent value, and a good breakfast is included in the price.

Imperial €€€€ *1, Kärntner Ring 16, tel: 01-50 100, fax: 01-501 0410, www.starwoodhotels.com.* Official guests of state, actors and leading popstars stay in the Imperial, with its 128 elegant rooms and suites. Definitely the place to be seen, and the restaurant is one of the best and most expensive in Vienna (the café isn't bad either). All rooms can accommodate guests with wheelchairs.

König von Ungarn €€€ 1, *Schulerstrasse 10, tel: 01-515 840, fax: 01-515 848, www.kvu.at.* Centrally located only metres from the Stephansdom, and over 400 years old, this hotel is full of old-fashioned charm. It has everything you would expect of a four-star hotel, and the glass-roofed inner courtyard is particularly attractive. All rooms are wheelchair-friendly and guests with cycles have access to repair and storage facilities.

Mailbergerhof €€€ 1, *Annagasse 7, tel: 01-512 0641, fax: 01-5120 64110, www.mailbergerhof.at.* An old building once belonging to the Knights Hospitallers with a modern interior, in the pedestrian area of the city centre. A full breakfast is included.

Meridien €€€€ 1, *Opernring 13, tel: 01-588 900, fax: 01-5889 09090, www.vienna.lemeridien.com.* Five-star luxury in a row of converted Ringstrasse buildings. The interiors have been beautifully designed, with clean modern lines. The restaurants are pretty good as well.

Nossek €–€€ 1, *Graben 17, tel: 01-533 7041, fax: 01-535 3646, www.pension-nossek.at.* Small, cosy pension in the heart of Vienna's shopping district. Credit cards are not accepted and reservations are highly recommended in the high season. Also available is an apartment for those wishing to stay longer.

Palais Coburg €€€€ 1, *Coburgbastei 4, tel: 01-518 180, fax: 01-518 181, www.palais-coburg.at.* Horribly expensive but wonderfully opulent, this mid-19th-century palace has been converted into a series of luxury suites. Everything is, as you would expect, very smooth, with a good restaurant, pool and city centre garden.

Pertschy €€ 1, *Habsburgergasse 5, tel: 01-534 490, fax: 01-534 4949, www.pertschy.com.* A friendly small hotel right in the middle of the Innere Stadt. The rooms are very comfy and pleasant in a kitschy Viennese sort of way (which is all part of the charm) and breakfast is included in the cost.

Radisson Palais €€€€ 1, *Parkring 16, tel: 01-515 170, fax: 01-512 2216, www.vienna.radissonsas.com*. Set in two Ringstrasse-era palaces, this impressive luxury conversion seeks to retain a Viennese flavour, which is generally successful even in the business-like rooms. The public areas are perhaps with best, with the entrance lobby particularly attractive.

Radisson Style Hotel €€€ 1, *Herrengassse 12, tel: 01-227 800, fax: 01-227 8077, www.vienna.radissonsas.com*. Very central, chic and well-designed, this modern 'style' hotel is a great place to stay. The rooms are very comfortable and the facilties excellent. Plus, it is not quite as expensive as it first appears (check out their 'specials' on the website).

The Ring €€€ 1, *Kärntner Ring 8, tel: 01-22122, fax: 01-2212 2900, www.theringhotel.com*. Opened in 2007, this cool but comfy Ringstrasse hotel has been given a cosy designer interior. The good-value classy rooms have a gently modern look, there is a great bar with an extensive wine list, and the hotel has a good day spa with the usual facials and massages.

Sacher €€€€ 1, *Philharmonikerstrasse 4, tel: 01-514 560, fax: 01-5145 7810, www.sacher.com*. Archdukes, ministers and senior army officers used to stay here, and the Sacher is still the city's most famous hotel. Past its heyday, perhaps, but you can still be sure of top-class service. Some rooms are accessible to wheelchair users.

Suzanne €€ 1, *Walfischgasse 4, tel: 01-513 2507, fax: 01-513 2500, www.pension-suzanne.at*. Two generations of the Strafinger family have been working to provide a pleasant stay in their spacious apartments with *fin-de-siècle*-style furnishings. The pension is close to the Opera and city centre.

Wandl €€–€€€ 1, *Petersplatz 9, tel: 01-534 550, fax: 01-534 5577, www.hotel-wandl.com*. Located immediately behind the Peterskirche (just off Graben), and thus very much at the hub of things. It was built in the 1700s as the residence of a court official, and still retains a historic feel. It has nice rooms and, for the facilities on offer, moderate rates.

Zur Wiener Staatsoper €€ 1, *Krugerstrasse 11, tel: 01-5131 2740, fax: 01-5131 27415, www.zurwienerstaatsoper.at*. Newly renovated and, as its name suggests, close to the opera. Small rooms, most with en-suite facilities, all facing a quiet, residential street. Advance reservations are recommended.

AROUND THE RINGSTRASSE (DISTRICTS 2–9)

Altstadt €€ 7, *Kirchengasse 41, tel: 01-522 6666, fax: 01-523 4901, www.altstadt.at*. Cool, modern and non-smoking rooms in a great *fin-de-siècle* building. Communal areas are decorated with contemporary works of art and the hotel is within easy walking distance of the MuseumsQuartier.

Biedermeier im Sünnhof €€€ 3, *Landstrasser Hauptstrasse 28, tel: 01-716 710, fax: 01-7167 1503, www.dorint.com*. A unique, attractive set of restored Biedermeier-style buildings, with original shopping arcade. It has specially outfitted rooms for guests with disabilities.

Das Triest €€€ 4, *Wiedner Hauptstrasse 12, tel: 01-589 180, fax: 01-589 1818, www.dastriest.at*. This great little design hotel set the scene for the explosion of chic, modern places to stay in Vienna. An old stable, dating back some 300 years, was given a new look by Terence Conran producing a, by now, characteristic mix of beautifully lit minimalist rooms and restored elements of the original building. There is a decent Italian restaurant and a great bar.

Das Tyrol €€–€€€ 6, *Mariahilfer Strasse 15, tel: 01-587 5415, fax: 01-587 54159, www.das-tyrol.at*. This boutique hotel close to the Museums Quartier has comfortable, low-key rooms in pretty greens and yellows. With a nod towards a designer feel it is an attractive but not over-the-top place to stay at a good price for the comfort and attentive service.

Haydn € *6, Mariahilfer Strasse 57–59, tel: 01-5874 4140, fax: 01-586 1950, www.haydn-hotel.at.* Simple, mid-range pension in a noisy area. Only a few minutes from the city centre by U-Bahn. There is cycle storage space available to guests, and breakfast is included.

The Imperial Riding School €€€ *3, Ungargasse 60, tel: 01-711 750, fax: 01-7117 58145, www.marriott.com.* One of the city's architecturally most striking hotels converted from riding stables built in 1850. It is slightly off the beaten track, about 10 minutes by tram from the Ringstrasse. All the comfortable but simple rooms can accommodate wheelchair users. As well as a lavish reception area there is a nice indoor pool.

Kugel € *7, Siebensterngasse 43, tel: 01-5233 3550, fax: 01-5233 3555, www.hotelkugel.at.* Good location in the middle of the shopping district, and small, clean rooms. Enthusiastic owners make the experience more enjoyable. Some rooms are outfitted for wheelchair use.

Levante Parliament €€€ *8, Auerspergstrasse 9, tel: 01-228 280, fax: 01-228 2828, www.thelevante.com.* A fantastic design hotel just behind the Parliament, parallel to the Ringstrasse. Set in a building from 1908, orginally designed by Secession architect Robert Oerley, the 2006 redesign featuring chic and cosy reds, browns and oranges, as well as specially commissioned photographs by Curt Themessl and glass sculptures by Ioan Nemtoi (for sale if you take a fancy to them), chimes in well with the orginal fabric of the building. The rooms and bathrooms themselves are very comfortable and elegant and the lovely interior courtyard is a great place for a drink or meal from the hotel's Nemtoi restaurant. In the basement is a relaxing sauna and 'wellness' area.

Hotel Rathaus Wien €€ *8, Lange Gasse 13, tel: 01-400 1122, fax: 01-4001 12288, www.hotel-rathaus-wien.at.* Inexpensive quiet rooms right in the middle of the lively Josefstadt district, with its many small bars. Each of the well-designed rooms is named after an Austrian wine maker, and samples of their wines are found in the minibar.

Wild € 7, *Lange Gasse 10, tel: 01-4065 1740, fax: 01-402 2168, www.pension-wild.com.* A popular pension in the Josefstadt district with large modern and very clean rooms with or without en-suite facilities, leading off a central stairwell. There are kitchenettes on every floor for light meals and a decent breakfast (included in the price) is served on the ground floor. A good, welcoming place to stay for gay and lesbian visitors.

FURTHER AFIELD

Klimt €€ 14, *Felbigergasse 58, tel: 01-914 5565, 01-911 1942, fax: 01-911 19425, www.klimt-hotel.at.* Renovated in a sort-of neo-*Jugendstil* style, this hotel offers the unusual option for guests to order special mattresses on request (a nice emphasis on a good night's sleep). It also has a fabulous honeymoon suite with canopied bed. Snack bar with meals available.

Landhaus Furhgassl-Huber €€ 19, *Rathstrasse 24, tel: 01-440 3033, fax: 01-440 2714, www.fuhrgassl-huber.at.* This hotel is at Neustift am Walde, an area of vineyards and *heuriger* within the city limits. Once the town hall, the fine interior was designed by Walter von Hoessl, one-time stage designer for the State Opera. It has comfortable rooms and is in a lovely, quiet location.

Parkhotel Schönbrunn €€€ 13, *Hietzinger Hauptstrasse 12, tel: 01-878 040, fax: 01-8780 43220, www.austria-trend.at.* Very close to the palace and gardens of Schönbrunn, this hotel formerly housed the emperor's guests and is still redolent of the Imperial past. Amenities include an indoor pool, satellite TV, and phones with voice mail as well as some rooms outfitted for wheelchair use. Rates include a generous breakfast.

The Rooms € 22, *Schlenthergasse 17, tel: 0664-431 6830, fax: 01-2636 70215, www.therooms.at.* This lovely bed and breakfast is a little way out of the centre in Donaustadt (near to Kagran U-bahn). Just three rooms (one single and two doubles), which are beautifully furnished, with views of the garden. Extremely good value but payment is in cash only.

Roomz € *11, Paragonstrasse 1, tel: 01-7431 777, fax: 01-7431 888, www.roomz-vienna.com.* Excellent value for a bit of modern comfort, this budget hotel near the Gasometers has spotless rooms with a designer feel, all with good bathrooms attached. There is a pleasant 24-hour bar and restaurant as well.

Schild €€ *19, Neustift am Walde 97–99, tel: 01-4404 0440, fax: 01-444 000, www.hotel-schild.at.* This 20-room hotel is a paradise for wine lovers, since it is surrounded by *Heurigen*. The country location is also appealing to cyclists as the hotel offers cycle storage and repair facilities. Wheelchairs are welcome in some rooms.

Sophienalpe € *14, Sofienalpenstrasse 13, tel: 01-486 2432, fax: 01-485 165 512, www.sophienalpe.at.* A country hotel, 20km (12 miles) from the centre, originally built by Franz Joseph as a summer house for his mother, Duchess Sophie. It offers good food, comfy rooms and a pool, and is an absolute bargain.

GUMPOLDSKIRCHEN

Benediktinerhof € *Kirchengasse 3, tel: 02252-62185, fax: 02252-6218 533, www.benediktinerhof.at.* This historic building, parts of which date back to 1549, is built around an attractive *Hof*, or courtyard. The pleasant, slightly old fashioned, rooms are large and very comfortable, and the hotel's wine bar and restaurant has some excellent local food and drink. There is even a small pool.

Hotel Turmhof €€ *Josef Schöffel Strasse 9, tel: 2252-607 333, fax: 2252-607 3336, www.hotel-turmhof.at.* This modern make-over of a pretty old building makes for attractive large rooms with spacious bathrooms. Most rooms have views over the surrounding vineyards and there is a great rooftop sauna.

Winzerhotel Vöhringer € *Wienerstrasse 26, tel: 02252-607 400, fax: 02252-607 4009, www.winzerhotel.at.* A very well-maintained small hotel with spotless rooms decorated in a modern style. The bathrooms are large and there is a lovely courtyard to sit out in. It is only five minutes' walk to the station into Vienna.

Recommended Restaurants

Dining out has always been a popular pastime in Vienna. It is part of Austrian culture to take the family out for lunch at the weekend and to meet friends in a *Beisl* (convivial Viennese equivalent of the bistro) or at the *Heuriger* wine garden. In restaurants, the emphasis is on good company, good wine, robust portions and, usually, reasonable prices for the quality of the ingredients – a dramatically different approach from many other European capitals.

When choosing a restaurant, something to bear in mind during the summer months is whether you can sit outside in a garden or *Schanigarten* (tables on the pavement with sunshades). If you're simply after a quick snack, then look for a traditional *Würstelstand*, a small kiosk selling sausages and other local specialities, such as *Leberkäsesemmel* (liver pâté sandwich). These kiosks are open almost all day and are to be found on street corners all over the city (see page 92).

Restaurants are listed alphabetically. Price categories are based on the cost, per person, of a dinner comprising starter, mid-priced main course and dessert (not including wine, coffee, or service) and are indicated as follows:

€€€	over 40 euros
€€	15–40 euros
€	15 euros and under

Cafés serve meals in the $ category unless otherwise specified.

RESTAURANTS

THE INNERE STADT (DISTRICT 1)

Artner am Franziskanerplatz €€–€€€ *1, Franziskanerplatz 5, tel: 01-503 5034, open daily 10am–2am, www.artner.co.at.* Sister restaurant to the more experimental Artner in the 4th district, this has some wonderful Austrian dishes, including regional specialities from Styria and good Burgenland wines, served in an atmospheric brick-lined cellar with some chic interior design.

Beim Czaak €–€€ *1, Postgasse 15, tel: 01-513 7215, open Mon–Sat 11am–midnight.* A friendly *Beisl* with helpful staff tucked away behind the Old University, and so popular with students. There is good food, particularly the *Tafelspitz*, sinful desserts and an excellent selection of beers.

Cantinetta Antinori €€–€€€ *1, Jasomirgottstrasse 3–5, tel: 01-5337 7220, open daily 11.30am–midnight, www.antinori.it.* Run by the famous Tuscan wine-producing family this is a slick Italian restaurant serving reliable food. Closely packed tables are not for non-smokers or the shy but do try the Chianti wines produced by the owners.

Coburg €€€ *1, Coburgbastei 4, tel: 01-5181 8800, open daily 7pm–midnight, www.palais-coburg.com.* One of the best places to eat in the city, in a very classy palace hotel. Opened in 2002 by chef Christian Petz, the Coburg dishes up great Austrian classics with a twist, and there is an amazing selection of wines (the cellar has over 50,000 bottles).

Esterhazy Keller € *1, Haarhof 1, tel: 01-533 3482, open Mon–Fri 11am–11pm, Sat–Sun 4–11pm.* A *Stadtheurigen* in a dark cellar; take the winding stairs down from the small doorway. Typical gut-busting food and local wines. Fine and atmospheric in a very Viennese sort of way.

Figlmüller €€ *1, Wollzeile 5, tel: 01-512 6177, open daily 11am–10.30pm, www.figlmueller.at.* Most famous for its *Wienerschnitzel* but now excessively touristy. However, the *Schnitzel* are certainly large, and tasty, and the wine is excellent.

Griechenbeisl €€ *1, Fleischmarkt 11, tel: 01-533 1977, open daily 11.30am–11.30pm, www.griechenbeisl.at.* This tavern was first recorded in 1447 and its small vaulted rooms have been a public house ever since. First frequented by Levantine and Greek merchants (hence the name), who inhabited Fleishmarkt, it was subsequently visited by many famous musicians and writers. Now the classic Viennese food is largely served up to the tourists who flock here.

Hansen €€ *1, Wipplingerstrasse 34, tel: 01-532 0542, open Mon–Fri 9am–11.30pm, Sat 9am–5pm, www.hansen.co.at.* Set in the vaulted cellars underneath Theophil Hansen's Borse building, and sharing the space with the florist Lederleitner, this is a lovely place for a meal. The food is modern Mediterranean with a slight Austrian twist and it is a great place for breakfast (served until 11.30am).

Hollmann Salon €–€€ *1, Im Heiligenkreuzerhof, Grashofgasse 3, tel: 01-9611 96040, open Mon–Sat 11am–10pm, www.hollmann-salon.at.* A delightful place to eat Viennese classics in one of Vienna's oldest squares. The minimalist décor of the white vaulted interior is chic and just a touch quirky (with songbirds mounted on the wall in one room). Most of the ingredients are organic and local, and the 'Quick-Slow-Food' lunchtime specials are great value (you pay what you like).

Hummerbar €€–€€€ *1, Mahlerstrasse 9, tel: 01-5128 8430, open Mon–Sat noon–midnight, www.hummerbar.at.* Said to be one of the best fish restaurants in Vienna, with a fresh catch flown in every day. Lobster is a speciality here, as are the fish soups.

Immervoll €–€€ *1, Weihburggasse 17, tel: 01-513 5288, open daily midday–midnight (kitchen closes 10.45pm).* A tiny, vaulted restaurant and café that has been carefully renovated. Popular at lunch time with local workers, it serves up lovely Viennese classics and has a good range of drinks.

Korso €€€ *1, Kärntner Ring 1, tel: 01-5151 6546, open Sun–Fri noon–3pm, 6pm–1am; closed Aug, www.restaurantkorso.at.* Taking the idea that Vienna has long been a culinary melting pot, Korso produces some of the best modern European cooking in town. Dishes range from cream soup with lobster ravioli to a roast saddle of vension with pumpkin, Jerusalem artichoke and barberries and there is a good selection of local wines.

Meinl's €€€ *1, tel: 01-5323 3346 000, open Mon–Wed 8.30am–midnight, Thur–Fri 8am–midnight, Sat 9am–midnight, www.*

meinlamgraben.at. Taking advantage of its place above Vienna's most prestigious food store, the eponymous Meinl. It serves up good reinvented Austrian classics and excellent wines.

Österreicher im MAK €€–€€€ *1, Stubenring 5, tel: 01-714 0121, open daily 11.30am–11.30pm, www.oesterreicherimmak.at.* The revamped café and restaurant of the Museum of Applied Arts has been beautifully designed and turns out excellent modern takes on Austrian classic dishes as well as a good selection of wines.

Palmenhaus €€ *1, Burggarten, tel: 01-533 1033, open daily, food served 10am–11pm, www.palmenhaus.at.* A spectacular Jugendstil glass house, now a restaurant and café. Good modern European dishes and a few Viennese classics although it can get quite crowded and noisy later on.

Pfudl €–€€ *1, Bäckerstrasse 22, tel: 01-512 6705, open daily 10am–11.30pm.* This *Beisl* has a rural atmosphere and finely prepared traditional Viennese cuisine, topped off with speedy service and a smallish bill.

Plachutta €€–€€€ *1, Wollzeile 38, tel: 01-512 1577, open daily 11.30am–midnight (kitchen closes 11.15pm), www.plachutta.at.* A long-standing central restaurant that is particularly famous for its *Tafelspitz* although the other Viennese classics are not bad either.

Reinthaler €–€€ *1, Dorotheergasse 4 and 1, Gluckgasse 5, tel: 01-512 1249/01-512 3366, open (Dorotheergasse) daily 11am–11pm, (Gluckgasse) Mon–Fri 9am–11pm.* Classic city centre *Beisln*, very popular with the Viennese for the hearty portions and quality of the food.

Trzesniewski € *1, Dorotheergasse 1, tel: 01-512 3291, open Mon–Fri 8.30am–7.30pm, www.trzesniewski.at.* With a great preserved interior this place specialises in the beloved Viennese open-faced sandwich, with toppings such as egg, red onion, salmon or crab. Diners cluster around chest-high tables and eat standing up; beer is the traditional drink here.

Wrenkh €€ *Bauernmarkt 10, tel: 01-533 1526, open Mon–Fri midday–4pm, 6–10pm, Sat 6–10pm, www.wiener-kochsalon.at.* A place for vegetarians and healthy eaters. First-class food, excellent wines and a cosy atmosphere.

Zu den 3 Hacken €–€€ *1, Singerstrasse 28, tel: 01-512 5895, open Mon–Sat 9am–midnight, closed public holidays, www.vinum-wien.at.* A good place for lovers of traditional Viennese cooking. The menu is big, and so are the portions. Very popular with the locals, so advance booking is essential.

Zu den drei Husaren €€€ *1, Weihburggasse 4, tel: 01-512 1092, open daily noon–3pm, 6pm–1am, www.drei-husaren.at.* Luxurious meals served by candlelight, complete with waltz music and a stylish interior. The starters and desserts are particularly recommended.

Zum Schwarzen Kameel € *1, Bognergasse 5, tel: 01-5338 1250, open Mon–Sat 8.30am–11.30pm, www.kameel.at.* Delicatessen and art nouveau restaurant that's full of history – allegedly Beethoven used to eat here – good for Viennese food.

Zwölf-Apostel-Keller €€ *1, Sonnenfelsgasse 3, tel: 01-512 6777, open daily 4.30pm–midnight, closed July, www.zwoelf-apostelkeller. at.* This well-known city-centre *Heuriger*, now a bit touristy, has an historic wine cellar on two floors, and serves good wines and hot (though average) food.

AROUND THE RINGSTRASSE (DISTRICTS 2–9)

Artner auf der Wieden €€–€€€ *4, Floragasse 6, tel: 01-503 5033, open Mon–Fri midday–midnight, Sat–Sun 6pm–midnight, www.artner.co.at.* There is perhaps a certain amount of style over substance at this chic, designer eatery, although the staff are friendly and there is a very good wine list. There is an emphasis on the degustation menus now so popular in Vienna's posher restaurants and certainly the artfully presented morsels of somewhat experimental dishes – made from first class ingredients – are very tasty.

Gasthaus Wild €€ *3, Radetzkyplatz 1, tel: 01-920 9477, open daily 10am–1am.* This *Beisl* has been beautifully restored, keeping the original character. The food, which includes typical Viennese dishes, is excellent, as is the selection of beers and wines.

Glacis Beisl €€ *7, Breitegasse 4, tel: 01-526 5660, open daily 11am–2pm, www.glacisbeisl.at.* Part of the MuseumsQuartier complex, a busy modern space that serves up great Viennese food. Very popular so you might want to book.

Schnattl €€€ *8, Lange Gasse 40, tel: 01-403 3400, open Mon–Fri 11.30am–2.30pm, 6–11pm, www.schnattl.com.* Superb modern Austrian dishes with fresh and delicate flavours. The interior is a pleasant and airy traditional space and the wines are excellent.

Schweizerhaus € *2, Prater 116, tel: 01-728 0152, open daily Mar–mid-Nov, 11am–midnight, www.schweizerhaus.at.* Huge portions of gut-busting roast pork knuckle (known as *Stelze*) served up in a very busy and popular eating house; you can also relax with a draught beer in the tree-shaded garden.

Silberwirt €–€€ *5, Schlossgasse 21, tel: 01-544 4907, open daily midday–midnight.* This very popular *Beisl* is packed at weekends with all kinds of people. Good, traditional dishes served up in a lovely courtyard, all at a decent price.

Steirereck im Wien €€€ *3, Am Heumarkt 2a, tel: 01-713 3168, open (restaurant) Mon–Fri midday–3pm, 7–10pm, (Meierei) Mon–Fri 9am–10pm, Sat 9am–11pm, Sun 9am–7pm, www.steirereck.at.* One of Austria's top restaurants, now relocated to a beautifully designed modern building overlooking the Stadtpark. It specialises in creative twists on Austrian classics. Try the cheaper lunch menu, or sample the huge range of cheeses in the Meierei.

Witwe Bolte €–€€ *7, Gutenberggasse 13, tel: 01-523 1450, open daily 11.30am–midnight.* Viennese home cooking in one of the city's oldest and most basic *Beisln*. In the interesting Spittleberg district.

Zum Altes Fassl €–€€ 5, *Ziegelofengasse 37, tel: 01-544 4298, open Sun–Fri 11.30am–3pm, 6pm–1am, Sat 6pm–1am, www.zum-alten-fassl.at.* Beisl featuring *al fresco* eating in atmospheric court-yards and garden. The classic Viennese food is excellent.

FURTHER AFIELD

Braunsperger €–€€ 19, *Sieveringer Strasse 108, tel: 01-320 3992, open daily Jan and alternate months 3pm–midnight.* If you have a particular interest in genuine local grape varieties, then don't miss this *Heuriger. Weissburgunder, roter Zweigelt* and *Grüner Veltliner* are among those on offer, while *Gemischter Satz* is a blend of different grape varieties that are picked and pressed together.

Fuhrgassl-Huber €–€€ 19, *Neustift am Walde 68, tel: 01-440 1405, open Mon–Sat 2pm–midnight, Sun, holidays noon–midnight, www.fuhrgassl-huber.at.* If you fancy a rustic setting, don't miss the earthy atmosphere of this *Heuriger.* On days when it's too cold to sit outside in the magnificent garden, warm yourself indoors with a plate of suckling pig, grilled chicken or other choice items from the buffet.

Gerhard Klager €–€€ 21, *Stammersdorfer Strasse 14, tel: 01-292 4107, open daily 1pm–midnight, every other month.* This *Heuriger* is particularly good for children, who can play in the playground while the adults sample fine wines and high-quality food. If you're driving, try the delicious low-alcohol grape must.

VIENNESE CAFÉS

Aida 1, *Stock–im–Eisen–Platz 2, tel: 01-512 2977, open Mon–Fri 6.30am–8pm, Sat 7am–8pm, Sun 9am–8pm.* Aida is a chain themed in shocking pink with 1950s décor. The coffee is wonderful (some say the best) and the *patisserie* is a dream.

Alt Wien 1, *Bäckerstrasse 9, tel: 01-512 5222, open Sun–Thur 9.30am–2am, Fri–Sat 9.30am–4am.* A café bordering on a *Beisl* with a deliberately decadent and dingy atmosphere. It offers a mouth-watering selection of snacks. You may come across an interesting literary clientele in the evenings.

Bräunerhof *1, Stallburggasse 2, tel: 01-512 3893, open Mon–Fri 7.30am–8.30pm, Sat 7.30am–6pm, Sun 10am–6pm.* Popular city-centre café with a wide selection of *Torten*.

Café Central *1, Herrengasse 14 (Palais Ferstel), tel: 01-533 3764 24, open Mon–Sat 8am–10pm, Sun 10am–6pm, holidays 10am–6pm.* The haunt of artists and intellectuals from times past, including Leon Trotsky and Peter Altenberg. Now touristy and pricey.

Café Drechsler *6, Linke Wienzeile 22, tel: 01-587 8580, open 3.30am–8pm.* This café has been providing hot beverages to the market traders across the road for years. The food is good and so are the prices.

Demel k.u.k Hofzuckerbäcker *1, Kohlmarkt 14, tel: 01-535 1717, open 10am–7pm.* Candies, crowds and cakes since 1796. Demel was, by appointment, pastry chef to Franz Joseph. It serves some of the best cakes in town.

Diglas *1, Wollzeile 10, tel: 01-5125 7650, open 7am–midnight.* An old coffee house with very comfortable seats and huge *Torten*. One of the best in the city, near Stephansplatz.

Frauenhuber *1, Himmelpfortgasse 6, tel: 01-512 4323, open Mon–Sat 8pm–midnight, Sun 10am–10pm.* One of Vienna's oldest cafés (1824) and one of the prettiest. It's said that Mozart performed here and Beethoven was a regular.

Griensteidl *1, Michaelerplatz 2, tel: 01-5352 6920, open 8am–11pm.* Light and airy café in traditional style, by the Hofburg.

Hawelka *1, Dorotheergasse 6, tel: 01-512 8230, open Mon, Wed–Sat 8am–2am, Sun 4pm–2am.* A rather dark and central café formerly patronised by artists.

Kleines Café *1, Franziskanerplatz 3, no telephone, open daily 10am–2am.* As the name suggests this is a tiny place, but beautifully designed and popular with local intellectuals. There is overspill outside in the square during summer.

Landtmann *1, Karl-Lueger-Ring 4, tel: 01-241 000, open 7.30am– midnight.* Always the most prestigious of the Ringstrasse cafés, next door to the Burgtheater.

Mozart *1, Albertinaplatz 2, tel: 24 10 00, open 8am–midnight.* There's been a café here since 1794. In Biedermeier times it was a meeting place for artists.

Museum *1, Friedrichstrasse 6, tel: 01-586 5202, open 8am–midnight.* Popular with arts students and lecturers, with a disastrously over-renovated Alfred Loos interior.

Prückel *1, Stubenring 24, tel: 512 61 15, open 8.30am–10pm.* Situated opposite the Museum of Fine Arts, this is a fine old Viennese café, with a 1950s interior, serving a full menu.

Schottenring *1, Schottenring 19, tel: 315 33 43, open Mon–Fri 6.30am–11pm, Sat–Sun 8am–9pm.* Founded in 1879, this café combines ancient and modern with live music, wonderful desserts and internet access.

Sperl *6, Gumpendorfer Strasse 11, tel: 586 41 58, open Mon–Sat 7am–11pm, Sun 11am–8pm.* Popular with Franz Lehár, and the meeting place of the stars, Sperl still attracts theatre people and literary types. Billiards and card tables.

Ubl *4, Pressgasse 26, tel: 01-587 6437, open noon–2.30pm, 6pm– midnight.* Old-fashioned establishment serving good *Schnitzels* and other classic fare such as *Zwiebelrostbraten* and *Tafelspitz*.

Zum Kapuziner *1, Neuer Markt 2, tel: 512 92 02, open 11am– midnight.* Opposite the Imperial Burial Vault, this comfortable establishment offers specialities such as beef goulash and roast duck.

INDEX

Berlitz pocket guide

Vienna

Ninth Edition 2009

Written by Jack Altman
Updated by Maria Lord
Series Editor: Tony Halliday

No part of this book may be reproduced, stored in a retrieval system or transmitted in any form or means electronic, mechanical, photocopying, recording or otherwise, without prior written permission from Berlitz Publishing. Brief text quotations with use of photographs are exempted for book review purposes only.

All Rights Reserved
© 2009 Berlitz Publishing/Apa Publications GmbH & Co. Verlag KG, Singapore Branch, Singapore

Printed in Singapore by Insight Print Services (Pte) Ltd, 38 Joo Koon Road, Singapore 628990. Tel: (65) 6865-1600. Fax: (65) 6861-6438

Berlitz Trademark Reg. U.S. Patent Office and other countries. Marca Registrada

Photography credits
AKG Images 40; Austria Tourism 13 (Trumler), 22 (Diejun), 28 (Bartl), 44, 49, 75 (Bohnacker), 76 (Krobath), 80 (Wiesenhofer), 81 (Herzberger), 84 (Kalmár), 89 (Bartl); Beryl Dhanjal; Glyn Genin 11, 27, 31, 46, 53, 54, 59, 64, 65, 66, 68, 69, 91, 93; Britta Jaschinski 24, 34, 36, 39, 55, 57, 63, 72, 79, 82, 87, 88, 95, 96, 97, 98; Maria Lord 35, 51; Museum D. Stadt Wien 17; iStockphoto 6, 7, 15, 19, 47, 48, 70, 86; Jupiter Images 33; Topham Picturepoint 20; Vienna Tourist Board 9, 42, 43.
Cover picture: 4Corners Images

Every effort has been made to provide accurate information in this publication, but changes are inevitable. The publisher cannot be responsible for any resulting loss, inconvenience or injury.

Contact us

At Berlitz we strive to keep our guides as accurate and up to date as possible, but if you find anything that has changed, or if you have any suggestions on ways to improve this guide, then we would be delighted to hear from you.

Berlitz Publishing, PO Box 7910, London SE1 1WE, England.
fax: (44) 20 7403 0290
email: berlitz@apaguide.co.uk
www.berlitzpublishing.com